Paul
Cézanne

By Richard Shiff

Rizzoli Art Series
Series Editor: Norma Broude

Paul Cézanne (1839–1906)

An Impressionist Touch

In memory of John Rewald, who gave the study of Cézanne its foundation

POPULAR HISTORIES describe Paul Cézanne as a pivotal figure who turned nineteenth-century painting away from Impressionist naturalism toward various forms of expressive abstraction—Paul Gauguin's symbolism, Henri Matisse's Fauvism, Pablo Picasso's cubism. Such accounts imply that Cézanne consciously pursued this direction, although his recorded statements are quite ambiguous and he openly ridiculed the symbolist and expressionist styles of his younger admirers. Perhaps the direction of the "influence" historians claim to have operated between the artist and his followers should be reversed: If Cézanne's paintings affected the course of twentieth-century art, it was not by his intention, but because his early champions determined how his art would subsequently be viewed. His followers interpreted Cézanne to make him seem their predecessor; they consciously created the authority or source they needed for their own position, claiming to discover it in a neglected master of the immediate past.

Most historians still associate Cézanne with the beliefs of his followers rather than with the practices of his own generation; they view his painting as if it were a product of the early twentieth century rather than the late nineteenth, displacing it chronologically. Cézanne's own psychology contributed to this curious situation. Because he was heir to his father's banking fortune, he knew his future promised material security; yet because he doubted the merits of his art, he never experienced emotional security. This set of circumstances may account for Cézanne's reluctance to cultivate a market for his work. He began to exhibit his paintings regularly only in 1895, at age fifty-six, having been prodded by the ambitious dealer Ambroise Vollard. When his work finally reached its public late in his life, it seemed to belong to a younger generation.

Perhaps Cézanne's isolation was for him a necessity—observers described the aging artist as reclusive, volatile, and even paranoid. In 1894 Claude Monet noted that Cézanne seemed "afraid to see new faces," while Monet's friend, the critic Gustave Geffroy provided a more elaborate characterization: "a person at once unknown and famous, having only rare contacts with the public and taken up as an influence among dissatisfied [painters], known only to some, living in determined isolation, reappearing, disappearing abruptly before the eyes of his intimates."[1] One young acquaintance suspected that Cézanne was shrewd enough to have dissembled: "He often exaggerated the strangeness of his conduct in order to protect his freedom. . . . The slightest intimacy seemed dangerous to him."[2]

Such documents portray an artist in psychological need of anonymity. Indeed, Cézanne's works remained unsigned—in the artist's mind, unfinished—unless a friend or patron wished to purchase one. It was Vollard together with Cézanne's son who selected works to be shown to the public, and there is no clear record indicating whether Cézanne actually attended his Paris exhibitions. Who, then, enjoyed the contact Cézanne clearly sought to avoid, a lasting familiarity with either the man or his art? Perhaps only his immediate family; yet a number of others knew the painter well at different times and have become especially important witnesses for historians.

Born in 1839, Cézanne spent his childhood in Aix-en-Provence in the south of France, where his schoolmate was Emile Zola. The two friends studied both writing and painting, were attracted to uncompromising realism as the style best suited to representing modernity, and dreamed of careers in Paris. During the late 1860s Zola succeeded in the literary field as both naturalist novelist and avant-garde art critic; but Cézanne, whose very direct manner of painting (see plate 1) seemed excessively crude to most viewers, remained a marginal figure—in Zola's eyes, a genius unrealized. Cézanne's true companions in painting were the Impressionists, including Monet, Pierre-Auguste Renoir, and Camille Pissarro: he exhibited with them three times during the 1870s (to little notice), and they would later regard his mature work as closely related to their own. The Impressionists each inspired aspects of Cézanne's innovative use of color, yet his art was by no means derivative of theirs. In the end Cézanne's art became a model for Impressionists to emulate: When Monet, even at the height of his fame, suffered bouts of depression, a look at the Cézannes he owned would disturb him all the more, a reminder that he might never match his isolated colleague's odd perfection.[3]

After the Impressionists, some notable younger painters became intrigued by Cézanne. During the 1880s, Gauguin and Van Gogh; and during the 1890s, members of a generation still younger, among them Emile Bernard and Maurice Denis, who eventually gathered anecdotal material while visiting the artist at his studio in Aix-en-Provence. According to this group of supporters, Cézanne had rightfully abandoned the initial principles of Impressionism: his work was converting objective appearance into subjective experience and attaining an image of universal significance beyond the sensation of the moment.

In 1907, a year after the painter's death, these grand philosophical issues were epitomized by Denis in a now famous statement. Cézanne, he wrote, was the "Poussin of impressionism." In the critical language of the time a reference to the seventeenth-century painter Nicolas Poussin signified the best of the old French tradition, the representation of nature in its ideal classical form. For Denis (as for many others who were advocating a return to traditional authority, not only in art but in religion and politics) "impressionism" connoted degenerate, undisciplined sensuality, a modern spontaneity without classical order. To become the "Poussin of impressionism" was, simply stated, to bring order back to an art of nature, a cultural gesture intended to save modern society from its individualist and anarchist excesses. Nevertheless, Denis did not believe that Cézanne's achievement derived from rational analysis of either painting technique, historical tradition, or contemporary social problems; instead he believed that his classicism came to him entirely naturally. In Denis's provocative phrasing, Cézanne's art was "spontaneously classical."[4]

To be spontaneous, natural, naive, and even primitive—to attain a classical order or ideal without being motivated by pretentious theories or petty professional ambitions—this was the substance of Cézanne's reputation during his final years. It all agreed with the fact of his irritability, unpredictability, and self-imposed isolation. He was reported to make such remarks as, "I'm the primitive of my own way" and "I do my thinking while I'm painting."[5] These statements appear to have been ironic responses to queries—Cézanne's way of discounting any need for historical precedent or a guiding aesthetic theory. According to witnesses and his letters to friends, Cézanne claimed to paint not from ideas but from feeling (what he called his personal "sensation" and "temperament"). He was so insistent about his direct, naive engagement with nature that he confused his equally insistent idealist followers. Having conversed with the master, a disappointed Bernard admitted to his mother in 1904, "Cézanne speaks only of painting nature according to his personality and not according to [the idea of] art itself. . . . He professes the theories of naturalism and impressionism."[6]

Cézanne's painting style, surely not his disconcerting words, must have offered what symbolist or idealist artists, along with the older Impressionists, found so immensely attractive. This style was complex in unexpected ways: it often combined discrete strokes of brilliant, primary color (an Impressionist technique) with bold, summary renderings of the human figure (evoking both classical motifs and the new symbolist art); critics often called the resultant forms "awkward." When Pissarro's friend Georges Lecomte assessed Cézanne's growing fame in 1899, he wondered whether the artist's pictorial awkwardness might actually have been a major cause of his unforeseen success. Lecomte reasoned that the Impressionists appreciated Cézanne's disregard for perspective and proportion because this signaled liberation from a long history of regulated academic practice—the artist was representing his sensations directly, allowing every idiosyncrasy. But the next generation brought history back into play. They compared Cézanne not to his formulaic academic predecessors but to more remote sources—the Italian "primitives," early Renaissance painters whose own awkwardly simple style was being sanctioned by symbolists as a model of naive purity. In view of the differing responses, Lecomte reached this startling conclusion: "At two successive stages in art [Impressionism and symbolism], Cézanne had the bizarre fortune of being lauded less for his qualities than for his faults [his awkwardness]."[7]

Many of the contradictions in the record of Cézanne's reception—to some his art was faithful naturalism, to others calculated abstraction—stem from the interpretive irony Lecomte was clever enough to perceive. The reclusive painter's "faults" made him a cultural hero for groups holding widely divergent aesthetic, social, and political positions; accordingly, the critical response accommodated an unusual number of interpretive claims. Cézanne's style would eventually be drawn upon not only by both primitivists and classicists, expressionists and constructivists, but also (without moral misgivings) by both anarchists and royalists. All this despite the fact that Cézanne's inscrutable images rarely thematized modernity (as Pissarro's, Monet's, and Renoir's often did), nor did they express any obvious political or religious allegory (as did Gauguin's, Bernard's, and Denis's). "Such is Cézanne," Denis concluded in 1920, "complex and diverse, that each one expects from him the confirmation of his own system."[8]

What, precisely, were Cézanne's "faults"? Certainly his figures were "awkward" by prevailing standards: "His nudes are never academic studies . . . what ignorance!" exclaimed one critic, actually applauding the distortions because they seemed naive and honestly felt.[9] Whether in appreciation or dismay, it was often stated that the artist's compositional motifs determined the form of his figures with surprising insistence, as when striding bathers assumed the linear rigidity of adjacent trees, to establish an abstract rhythmical order (see plates 9 and 16). The artificiality of these groupings of bathers and landscape elements is in part explained by the fact that Cézanne avoided using live models. Instead he combined individual figures derived from his own numerous sketches after works in the Louvre and reproductions in art books; sometimes he radically altered the anatomy, rendering it improbable or even changing the sex.

To attribute the cause of such figural and thematic conundrums to emotionally expressive "distortion" and a liberated sense of form became central to an expressionist mode of interpretation developed early in the twentieth century. Matisse, who purchased Cézanne's *Three Bathers* (plate 9) in 1899, said later of his own painting style that the demands of immediate expression determined "the entire arrangement . . . the position occupied by solid bodies, the empty spaces surrounding them, the proportional relationships."[10] And in 1912 Wassily Kandinsky, who was developing an abstract art, claimed that in the *Large Bathers* (plate 16) Cézanne "distorts the human figure justifiably. Not only must the whole figure follow the lines of the triangle, but each limb is driven upward, as it were, becoming ever lighter and more expansive."[11] British critic Roger Fry had a similar response, characteristic of his emphasis on the play of form: "At any moment [in Cézanne's working process] the demand of the total construction for some vehement assertion of a rectilinear direction may do violence to anatomy."[12]

Anatomy was not the only site of willful expression; critics also wondered how to distinguish foregrounds from backgrounds and rounded volumes from flat planes, because Cézanne would often paint the flat patterns of tablecloths and wallpapers with an intensity and vigor equal to that of rounded vases or pieces of fruit. His *Fruit Bowl, Glass, and Apples* (plate 8) thus includes a visual pun: the leaves of the wallpaper pattern appear to project from the background plane and hover over the table and bowl; the viewer struggles to discern at what level of "reality" these leaves might exist—is the painter imitating an artifice of wall decoration or a form of organic life?

Similarly, Cézanne sometimes incorporated parts of his own works into backgrounds. His *Peasant in a Blue Smock* (plate 11) appears to include a woman with a parasol emerging from the distance, but this is in fact an image from a painted decorative screen the artist had created much earlier. And in *Still Life with Plaster Cupid* (plate 10) Cézanne allowed the "real" patterned cloth that forms part of his foreground table arrangement (a prop he used many times) to merge with a version of the same cloth, part of another painting seen in process in his studio. Still more confusing, Cézanne arranged his complex composition so that the sculpted foreground Cupid is set pictorially against a blank canvas lying along the background wall, as if to suggest that the Cupid might have been painted on canvas rather than cast in plaster—which, in the most literal sense, is actually the case, since the entire surface of this still-life composition has indeed been painted. Cézanne's viewer seems to witness the illusionistic sculptural quality of the plaster Cupid being converted (back) into a material surface of paint. The visual illusion reveals its own source in a tactile medium, oil pigment.

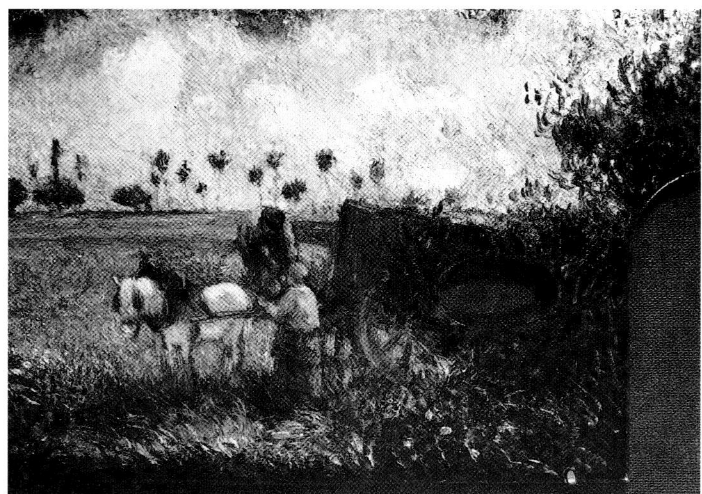

1. Camille Pissarro. *The Artist's Palette with a Landscape.* 1878. Oil on palette, 9½ x 13⅝". Sterling and Francine Clark Art Institute, Williamstown, Massachusetts

Given such disturbing fusions of elements that one would have expected to appear quite separate—"faults" by conventional standards of pictorial organization—viewers often concentrated on what could properly be seen as a totality, the effect of Cézanne's weave of vibrating color, a feature especially prominent in his later landscapes (plates 12, 13, 14, and 15). Several early critics compared this effect to tapestry, attributing it to the artist's use of contrasts of saturated hues in place of a nuanced chiaroscuro (gradated values of dark and light). With this type of color, wrote Denis, "the perspective planes disappear."[13] Indeed, during the 1870s and early 1880s, while working beside Pissarro in rural areas outside Paris, Cézanne developed a way of representing outdoor light by juxtaposing strokes of primary hues and their secondary combinations; this allowed the level of brightness to remain relatively uniform across the canvas (see plates 3 and 6). In a remarkable composition painted on an actual palette (fig. 1), Pissarro indicated how central it was to earlier Impressionist method (Cézanne's included) to limit the number of pigments from which all hues would be derived. This ensured that the individual colors, no matter how brilliant or jarring, would harmonize among themselves to produce a coherent light. Pissarro constructed his view of peasant workers by relying on combinations of the six pigments seen laid out along his picture's edges; the wooden palette supports both the constituent materials and the resultant image, demonstrating the artist's active construction of a painted light.

Cézanne employed a simplified range of pigments very similar to Pissarro's. During the 1870s he gradually brightened the general effect by reducing the number of mixed combinations and making more pronounced juxtapositions of contrasting colors (compare plates 4 and 5). The quality of unvarying light in Cézanne's paintings was antithetical both to atmospheric perspective and to dramatic indoor lighting. Even when painting indoors—whether a still life (plate 8), a portrait (plate 5), or an imaginary figure composition (plate 9)—Cézanne created the effect of uniform brightness he believed to be characteristic of full daylight. His purpose was twofold: he wished not only to represent what was "natural" (colors associated with daylight) but also to assert his own individual being; some called it his "temperament" or "personality," others his "originality" or "genius." "I paint as I see, as I feel," Cézanne once explained to a journalist, adding with irony, "and I have very strong sensations."[14]

The artist's goal of individual expression could only be reached by escaping the conventional practices that restricted painters to predetermined channels of communication. Yet it would be a mistake to conclude that Cézanne actually transcended the limits set by the artistic techniques acceptable during his era. Rather, he succeeded in representing for his generation the ideal or value of such transcendence. He did this by devising techniques that signified or connoted an individual's expressive freedom (and by extension, social and political independence). For example, he often reworked familiar pictorial themes (whether picturesque landscapes or old master compositions) with color patterns and schemes of proportion recognizably in violation of traditional studio practice. Although Cézanne's cultural icons may have seemed commonplace, the sensory effect of his style was not. When Denis labeled Cézanne the "Poussin of impressionism," he was attempting to reestablish the principle of art as a culturing or ordering of nature. But Cézanne's actions can just as easily be imagined to have inverted that principle: He was transferring his immediate, idiosyncratic sensation—of both external nature and his own nature—into a preexistent realm of art, perhaps producing more disorder than order. Certainly he created a fertile interpretive confusion.

Indeed, the particularities of Cézanne's technique were sufficiently multivalent to sustain the interest of those with whom he never felt much affinity. The fact of his ever-increasing influence found pictorial expression in Denis's painting *Hommage à Cézanne* (1900), which depicted a group of artists gathered around the master's *Fruit Bowl, Glass, and Apples,* a still life once owned by Gauguin, who had himself used it to explain Cézanne's principles.[15] Gauguin offered his own pictorial testament to Cézanne in a portrait (fig. 2) that had as its background this same still life (plate 8). His attention to Cézanne's style reveals yet another feature of the artist's practice that was meaningful to his early admirers: Gauguin carefully imitated the character of Cézanne's short, accentuated brush strokes, which he viewed as the mark of both a sensitive hand and an active mind. Compared with conventional painting practices, Cézanne's use of brilliantly colored, discrete strokes of pigment signified not only immediacy of vision (Impressionist naturalism) but also independence of action, an unconstrained gesture in resistance to standards for the refinement of pictorial surfaces.

If Cézanne's mark departed from expectations for depictions of nature as well as from the traditional craft of paint-

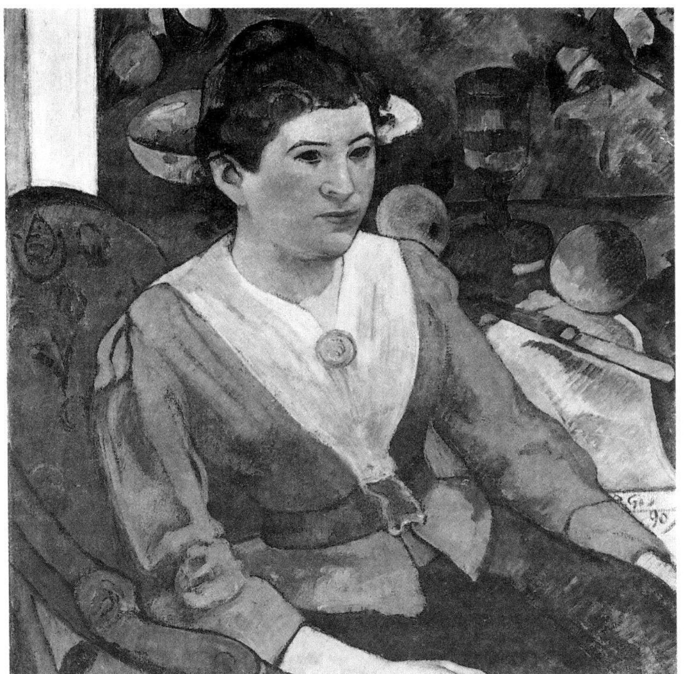

2. Paul Gauguin. *Portrait of a Woman, with Still Life by Cézanne.* 1890. Oil on canvas, 25¾ x 21⅔". The Art Institute of Chicago. Joseph Winterbotham Collection

ing, what did it communicate or express? For Gauguin and many others, the answer was expression itself: Cézanne's mark manifested a self actively engaged in sensation, emotion, and felt idea; the mark indexed thought in its most immediate form, thought made material and sensual ("Individuality shows itself in the brush stroke," stated a painter's manual of the time).[16] It was not a matter of a preconceived theme or meaning being described or pictured, but rather an ethic, a way of life activated in the experience of marking, coloring, and forming.

Such interpretation was actually consistent with the thinking of the Impressionists, despite differences perceived by members of Gauguin's generation. Renoir, for instance, appreciated the fact that Cézanne "had only to put a single stroke of color on a canvas for it to merit interest."[17] Indeed, fragmentary studies such as the one known variously as *Two and a Half Apples* and *Three Apples,* which measures only four inches wide (fig. 3), became prized possessions for collectors. The confusion over the title of this work is telling, for to consider it *Two and a Half Apples* is to give the mark precedence over whatever it might depict. Cézanne's marking ends with half an apple at the edge of the canvas itself (total: two and a half), whereas the pictorial illusion continues, leading the imagination beyond this framing edge to include a completed piece of fruit (total: three). For Renoir and others who concentrated on the material evidence of Cézanne's presence, his tiny *Two and a Half Apples* represented not pieces of fruit but a significant piece—some moments of experience—of the painter.

Visibly discrete brush strokes of the kind seen prominently in *Two and a Half Apples* and in many of Cézanne's portraits and landscapes (plates 5, 6, and 7) are commonly called "touches," because they result from acts of touching. By using this term, Cézanne's early observers, whether self-consciously or not, linked painting to the body; they turned criticism from discussion of narrative and thematic development to focus on painting's engagement of the hand and its significance for a direct experience of physicality—the body's sense of itself in relation to its material environment.

We usually encounter our own physicality as if, like "nature," it was already in place, its intimate presence revealed to us by whatever affects it, eliciting reaction or response. Yet we can also understand physicality as a dimension of human consciousness constructed in experience and therefore subject to change whenever the general character of experience itself may change (to pass from agrarian-village to industrial-urban forms of life, as so many did during the nineteenth century, constitutes such a transformation of experience). Twentieth-century theories of representation have argued that artistic production constructs physicality and subjectivity through an interaction of image and viewer (the image inducing in both artist and audience a certain self-imaging). If this point seems obscure, think of the way certain perspectives make a body feel closed in or uncomfortably large or small; or how one's body responds kinesthetically to the rhythm perceived in a pattern, whether man-made or found in nature; or how familiarity with handling and fashioning specific materials makes them seem part of oneself, part of human existence; or how observing another's act makes its execution seem realizable for oneself. Creative representation—the painting of a still life or a landscape—is a physical process that renders both artist-actor and critic-observer sensitive to the form a human life assumes as it articulates its own position of viewing and touching within a material environment.[18] As Cézanne's painting set an example of a certain level of concentrated seeing and personalized touching, it made that mode of sensory understanding possible for others.

Some of Cézanne's early critics gave special recognition to this physical aspect of his practice. When Geffroy reviewed the artist's first exhibition at Vollard's gallery, noting that most of the paintings lacked signatures and other signs of professional finish, he advised his reader, "Have no fear, the works are [indeed] signed, better marked than by a signature."[19] Geffroy meant that Cézanne's character was in each and every mark, and the mark could only be his. In a later review this critic went further, converting into a virtue

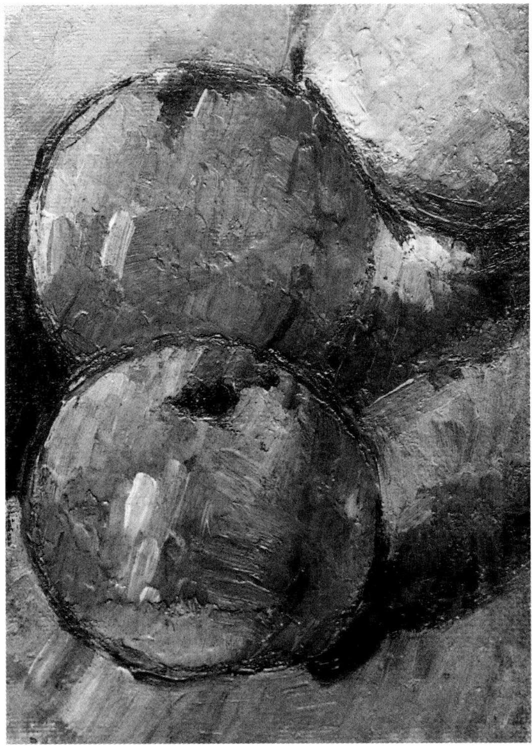

3. *Three Apples.* c. 1875–1878. Oil on canvas, 6½ x 3$^{15}/_{16}$". The Barnes Foundation. Photograph © copyright 1994 by The Barnes Foundation

the "fault" many were observing, the possibility that the marks failed to form a coherent representational image: "They say Cézanne's canvases are not finished. . . . [Yet] art does not proceed without a certain incompleteness, because the life it reproduces is in perpetual transformation."[20] Geffroy regarded each of the painter's marks as the representation of a moment of sensation and experience in an evolving organic world, a personalized record of a changing history of human subjectivity; others would live through such a history, but without an artist's acute perception. By Geffroy's characterization life's experience is unbounded and unpredictable; its appropriate image would therefore lack the completeness of conventionally composed pictures. The painter's action—which not only constructed but was also implicated in and responded to the picture as it emerged on the canvas—became a model for unrestricted experience. It represented in microcosm the ideal of a freely evolving society that nineteenth-century theorists of various political orientations were promoting. Geffroy's own anarchist beliefs accorded with such interpretation, whereas Cézanne simply attributed his incompletion to the difficulty of representing sensation in paint: "I cannot reach the intensity that opens up before my senses," he conceded not long before his death.[21]

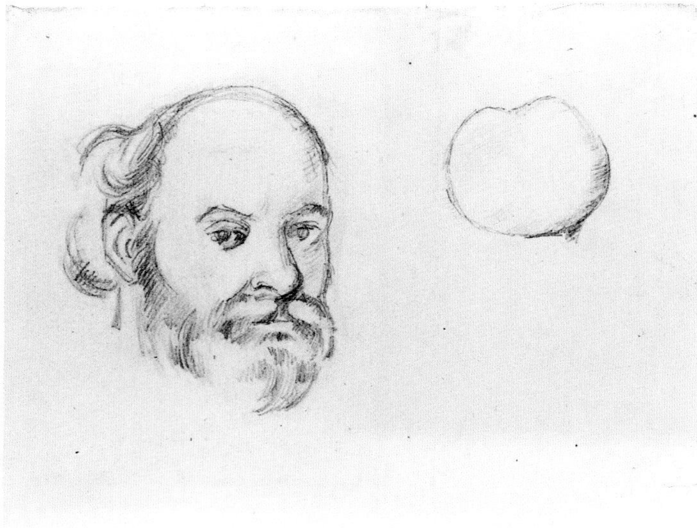

4. *Self-Portrait and Apple*. 1882–1883. Pencil drawing, 6⅞ x 9". Cincinnati Art Museum. Gift of Emily Poole

There is more to why Cézanne's "touch" satisfied a pattern of critical speculation built around the value of spontaneous expression, of authentic engagement with the material world by both eye and hand. Cézanne's surfaces typically consist of abruptly juxtaposed strokes, each distinguished from its neighbors but repetitive enough to establish continuity, with passages of color often extended across the proper boundaries of depicted objects—for instance, from foreground foliage to background sky (see plate 12). Cézanne tended to work laterally across the paper or canvas, connecting disparate features of the picture by a chain of formal analogies that respected the quality of the stroke itself (recall the way his bathers might resemble rectilinear trees).

Through analogy, one thing is made to look like, or somehow be like, another, despite the differences and dissimilarities that otherwise obtain. This principle is especially apparent in some of Cézanne's sketchbook drawings. In a self-portrait sheet (fig. 4) the artist not only implied a comparison between the form of an apple and his own skull, but included behind his head what appears to be an element of the back of a chair; this fragment extends the form of the head by repeating the motif of its contour. The observer cannot decide whether the artist is perceiving and recording visual patterns common to diverse materials (apple, head, chair) or whether an autonomous rhythm of the hand is determining the apprehension of form. Similarly, in a watercolor (fig. 5) Cézanne defined the contours of skulls with sets of curves that he also used to render the pattern of a decorative cloth. It would be misleading to attribute such formal analogy to an artist's simple observation of the visual effects of objects. Cézanne's image derives instead from a skillful act of expressive representation in which the hand moves along the surface of the paper, repeating or imitating gestures already made; the hand develops a motif belonging as much to the sense of touch as to a visual sense of the model. Critics like Geffroy might conclude that hand and eye are moving freely and in harmony, liberated from any restrictive hierarchy of the senses. Neither sense—touch, the more physical, vision, the more intellectual—dominates the other.

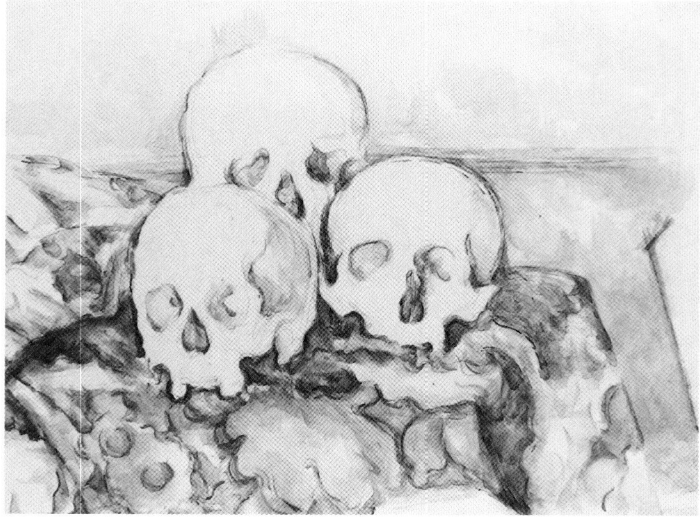

5. *Three Skulls*. 1902–1906. Watercolor, 18$\frac{7}{10}$ x 24¾". The Art Institute of Chicago. Mr. and Mrs. Lewis Larned Coburn Memorial Collection

Would the artist have agreed? Probably not in these precise words. Yet Cézanne's isolated determination to picture nature in relation to his individualized sensory and emotional experience seems in accord with the openness and revelatory expressiveness that critics attributed to his art, if not always to him.[22] Anxious over increasing mechanization and depersonalization of daily life, early modernist critics saw in Cézanne's visualizing touch the possibility of reexperiencing a primordial physicality. Many of today's social and cultural issues are analogous—we fear a standardization and deadening of sensation. Perhaps Cézanne's paintings continue to provoke because they present a discourse of the senses our theories still cannot contain.

NOTES

1. Claude Monet, letter to Gustave Geffroy, 23 November 1894, in Gustave Geffroy, *Claude Monet: Sa vie, son oeuvre* (Paris: Crès, 1924), Vol. II, p. 65; Gustave Geffroy, "Paul Cézanne" (1894), *La Vie artistique* (Paris: Dentu; Floury, 1892–1903), Vol. III, p. 249.
2. Edmond Jaloux, *Les Saisons littéraires 1896–1903* (Fribourg: Editions de la Librairie de l'Université, 1942), pp. 75–76. On Cézanne's character, see also John Rewald, *Cézanne, Geffroy et Gasquet* (Paris: Quatre Chemins-Editart, 1959); and Jean-Claude Lebensztejn, "Persistance de la mémoire," *Critique* 49 (August–September 1993), pp. 609–630.
3. As reported by Octave Mirbeau in 1906; see Maurice Denis, *Journal* (Paris: La Colombe, 1957–1959), Vol. II, p. 46.
4. Maurice Denis, "Cézanne," *L'Occident* 12 (September 1907), pp. 124, 132. Cf. Shiff, 1984, pp. 165–166, 180–183.
5. Pemberton, 1991 (1921), p. 155; Denis, 1957–1959, Vol. II, p. 29 (literally, Cézanne referred to "seeking" or "researching" while painting).
6. Emile Bernard, "Un Extraordinaire Document sur Paul Cézanne," *Art-Documents* 50 (November 1954), p. 4.
7. Georges Lecomte, "Paul Cézanne," *Revue d'art* 1 (9 December 1899), p. 86.
8. Maurice Denis, "L'Influence de Cézanne," *L'Amour de l'art* 1 (December 1920), p. 279.
9. Félicien Fagus, "Quarante tableaux de Cézanne," *La Revue blanche* 20 (1 September 1899), p. 627.
10. Henri Matisse, "Notes d'un peintre," *La Grande Revue* 52 (25 December 1908), p. 733.
11. Wassily Kandinsky, *Concerning the Spiritual in Art and Painting in Particular*, trans. M. Sadler (New York: Wittenborn, 1947 [1912]), p. 49.
12. Fry, 1989 (1927), p. 57.
13. Denis, 1907, p. 131.
14. See John Rewald, "Un Article inédit sur Paul Cézanne en 1870," *Arts*, Paris, 473 (21–27 July 1954), p. 8.
15. See Merete Bodelsen, "Gauguin, the Collector," *Burlington Magazine* 112 (September 1970), p. 606.
16. Félix Bracquemond, *Du dessin et de la couleur* (Paris: Charpentier, 1885), p. 151.
17. Auguste Renoir, quoted in Georges Rivière, *Cézanne, le peintre solitaire* (Paris: Floury, 1936), p. 19.
18. Cf. Maurice Merleau-Ponty, "Cézanne's Doubt" (1945), *Sense and Non-Sense*, trans. Hubert L. Dreyfus and Patricia Allen Dreyfus (Evanston, Ill.: Northwestern University Press, 1964), pp. 9–25.
19. Geffroy, "Paul Cézanne" (1895), in Geffroy, 1892–1903, Vol. I, p. 215.
20. Geffroy, "Salon de 1901" (1901), in Geffroy, 1892–1903, Vol. III, p. 376.
21. Paul Cézanne, letter to his son, 8 September 1906, in Rewald, 1978, p. 324.
22. In his later years Cézanne's political views became increasingly reactionary—for Geffroy a problem, for Denis a delight.

FURTHER READING

Adriani, Götz. *Cézanne, Gemälde.* Cologne: DuMont, 1993.

Andersen, Wayne. *Cézanne's Portrait Drawings.* Cambridge, Mass.: MIT Press, 1970.

Chappuis, Adrien. *The Drawings of Paul Cézanne.* Greenwich, Conn.: New York Graphic Society, 1973.

Doran, P. Michael, ed. *Conversations avec Cézanne.* Paris: Macula, 1978.

Fry, Roger. *Cézanne: A Study of His Development.* Chicago: University of Chicago Press, 1989 (1927).

Geist, Sidney. *Interpreting Cézanne.* Cambridge: Harvard University Press, 1988.

Gowing, Lawrence, ed. *Cézanne: The Early Years, 1859–1872.* New York: Harry N. Abrams, 1988.

Kendall, Richard, ed. *Cézanne & Poussin: A Symposium.* Sheffield: Sheffield Academic Press, 1993.

Krumrine, Mary Louise. *Paul Cézanne: The Bathers.* Basel: Museum of Fine Arts, 1989.

Lewis, Mary Tompkins. *Cézanne's Early Imagery.* Berkeley: University of California Press, 1989.

Pemberton, Christopher, trans. *Joachim Gasquet's Cézanne.* London: Thames and Hudson, 1991 (1921).

Reff, Theodore. "Cézanne and Poussin." *Journal of the Warburg and Courtauld Institutes* 23 (1960), pp. 150–174.

Rewald, John. *Cézanne: A Biography.* New York: Harry N. Abrams, 1986.

———, ed. *Paul Cézanne, Correspondance.* Paris: Grasset, 1978. English edition: *Paul Cézanne: Letters,* trans. Seymour Hacker. New York: Hacker, 1984.

———. *Paul Cézanne: The Watercolors.* Boston: New York Graphic Society, 1983.

Rubin, William, ed. *Cézanne: The Late Work.* New York: Museum of Modern Art, 1977.

Schapiro, Meyer. *Paul Cézanne.* New York: Harry N. Abrams, 1952.

Shiff, Richard. *Cézanne and the End of Impressionism.* Chicago: University of Chicago Press, 1984.

———. "Cézanne's Physicality." In Salim Kemal and Ivan Gaskell, eds. *The Language of Art History.* Cambridge: Cambridge University Press, 1991, pp. 129–180.

Venturi, Lionello. *Cézanne: Son art, son oeuvre.* 2 vols. Paris: Paul Rosenberg, 1936.

Verdi, Richard. *Cézanne and Poussin: The Classical Vision of Landscape.* Edinburgh: National Galleries of Scotland, 1990.

First published in 1994 in the United States of America by
Rizzoli International Publications, Inc.
300 Park Avenue South
New York, New York 10010

Library of Congress Cataloging-in-Publication Data

Shiff, Richard.
Paul Cézanne / by Richard Shiff.
p. cm. — (Rizzoli art series)
Includes bibliographical references.
ISBN 0-8478-1755-5
1. Cézanne, Paul, 1839–1906—Criticism and interpretation.
2. Impressionism (Art)—France. I. Title. II. Series.
ND553.C33S5 1994
759.4—dc20 94-14283
CIP

Designed by Brian Sisco
Series Editor: Norma Broude
Editor: Charles Miers
Assistant Editor: Cathryn Drake
Compositor: Rose Scarpetis

Front cover: see colorplate 16

Printed in Italy

Index to Colorplates

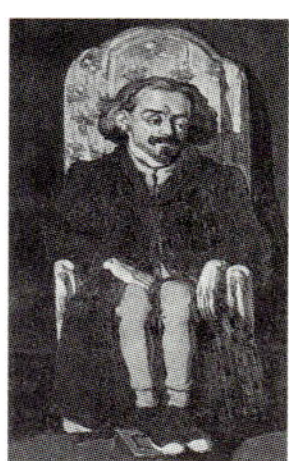

1. *Portrait of Achille Emperaire.* c. 1868–1870. This large-scale portrait of Cézanne's friend, the painter Achille Emperaire, complete with brilliantly colored robe, may have been intended to parody aggrandizing images such as Jean-Auguste-Dominique Ingres's portrait of Napoleon, another "emperor."

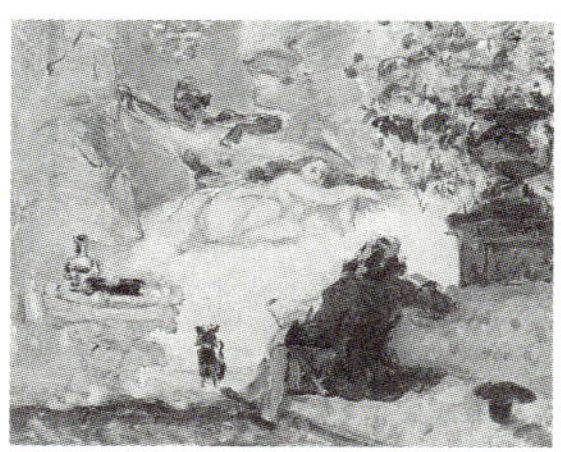

2. *A Modern Olympia.* 1873–1874. Cézanne chose this painting as one of only three works he exhibited with the Impressionists in 1874, presumably fully aware it would outrage the public. His "modern Olympia" parodies the art of Edouard Manet, whose own *Olympia*, the image of a prostitute, created a scandal at the Salon of 1865. Imagining himself in competition with Manet, Cézanne makes the theme of illicit (yet commonplace) sexuality all the more overt by including the gentleman client in the picture. His loose brushwork renders the style as "modern" as the provocative subject.

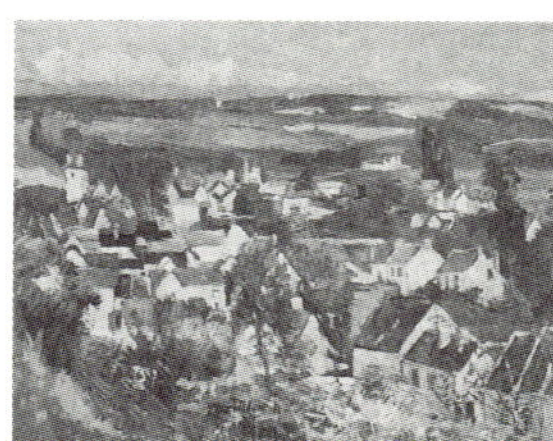

3. *Village of Auvers.* c. 1874. Painted in the agricultural region where Pissarro was also at work, this landscape is one of the earliest by Cézanne to rely so exclusively on the use of primary hues. Although it retains a degree of traditional atmospheric perspective (the distant parts of the landscape becoming relatively pale), all areas reveal a vigorous handling.

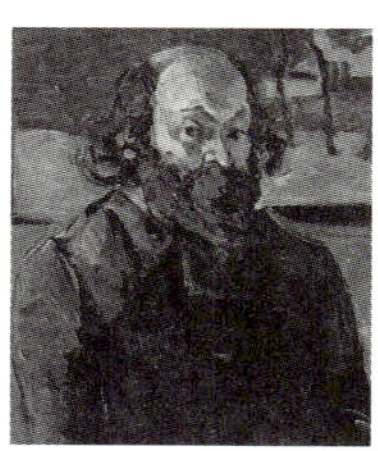

4. *Self-Portrait.* c. 1872. Blacks and grays predominate, yet individual brush strokes reveal traces of primary colors mixed in various combinations to create the facial tones. Cézanne painted this self-portrait in the studio of Armand Guillaumin, whose large cityscape is appropriately shown reversed in the mirrored background.

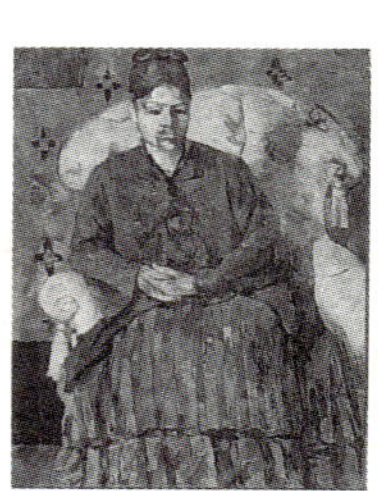

5. *Portrait of Mme Cézanne.* 1877–1878. Cézanne painted his wife, Hortense Fiquet, many times—often, it seems, with photographs, his own sketchbook drawings, or his previous paintings to guide him. In this relatively early version he models the face with tones of orange and green in a manner similar to that of the other Impressionists.

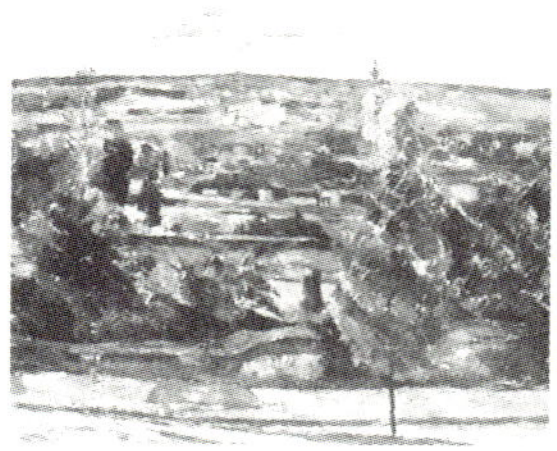

6. *Landscape (Near Melun?).* c. 1879–1882. A network of variously dense and loose brush strokes characterizes this brilliantly colored landscape. Groups of individual marks—diagonal, horizontal, vertical—record all changes in composition and indicate that Cézanne may have decided to eliminate a small tree at left of center.

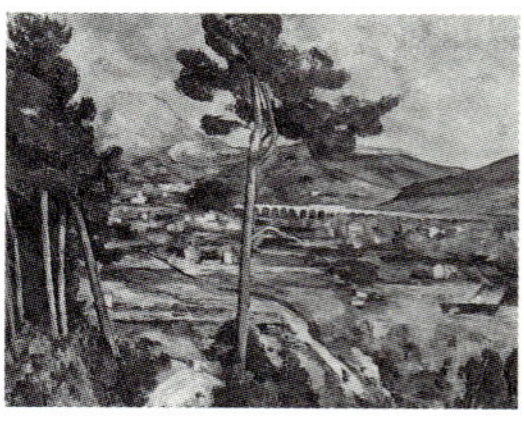

7. *Mont Sainte-Victoire.* c. 1883–1885. The view is taken from property occupied by the artist's sister; it shows the great curving viaduct on the railway from Marseille as it approaches Aix. The scale of Cézanne's brush strokes integrates the central pine tree with the pattern of cultivated fields in the valley.

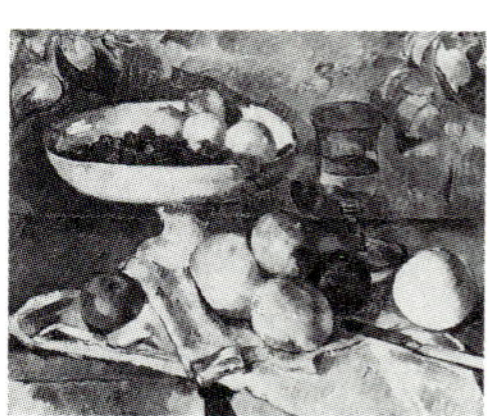

8. *Fruit Bowl, Glass, and Apples.* c. 1880. Gauguin was the proud owner of this painting during the 1880s; he sold it around 1897 only when he was desperate for money. A Polish painter visiting Paris in 1894 reported that Gauguin brought the painting to meetings of young artists to instruct them on Cézanne's methods.

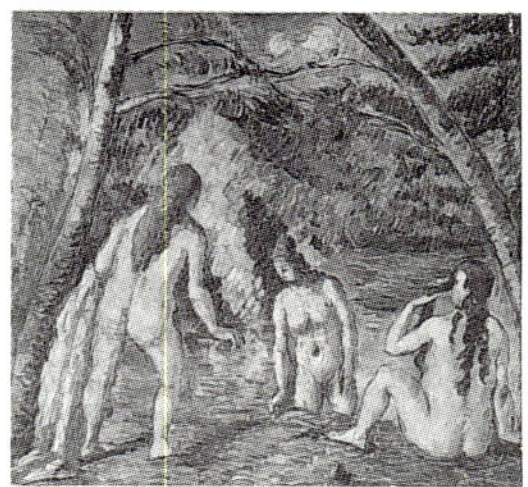

9. *Three Bathers.* c. 1881–1882. Matisse was so struck by this painting that he purchased it from Vollard's gallery even though it strained his finances; years later he offered it in tribute to the city of Paris. Sensitive to Cézanne's visual analogies, Matisse told an interviewer, "Everything there was in order, hands and trees counted in the same manner as the sky."

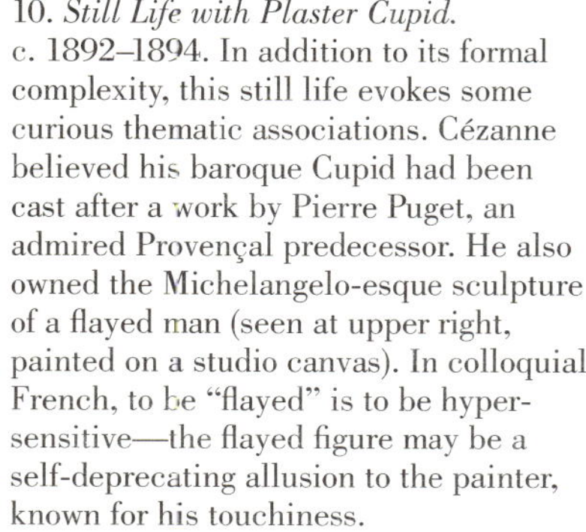

10. *Still Life with Plaster Cupid.* c. 1892–1894. In addition to its formal complexity, this still life evokes some curious thematic associations. Cézanne believed his baroque Cupid had been cast after a work by Pierre Puget, an admired Provençal predecessor. He also owned the Michelangelo-esque sculpture of a flayed man (seen at upper right, painted on a studio canvas). In colloquial French, to be "flayed" is to be hypersensitive—the flayed figure may be a self-deprecating allusion to the painter, known for his touchiness.

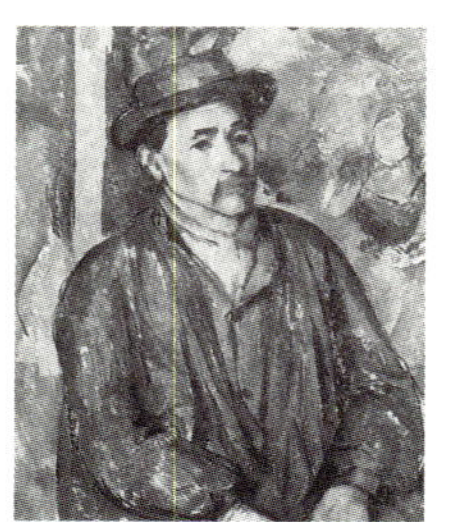

11. *Peasant in a Blue Smock.* c. 1897. Although Cézanne avoided the use of live models for his bathers, he was at ease with the local Provençal workers employed on his property, picturing them in various settings. Here the composition, as in several of his still lifes, includes as its background a fragment of a large decorative screen he had painted for his father's study around 1859–1860.

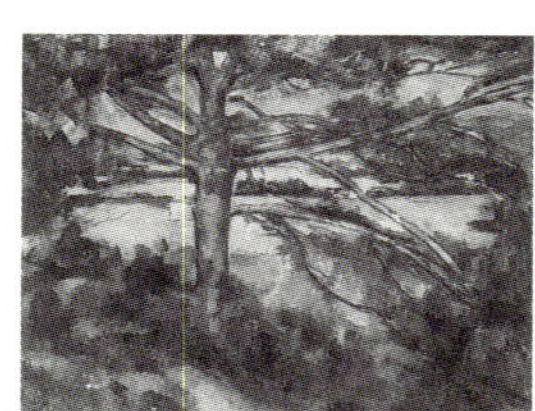

12. *Large Pine Tree near Aix.* c. 1895–1897. Cézanne painted this particular tree several times. He found the dense pine forests around Aix a congenial subject. presumably because they were characteristic of his beloved Provence. He often painted background strokes over individual branches, willfully confusing background and foreground as he would in his still lifes.

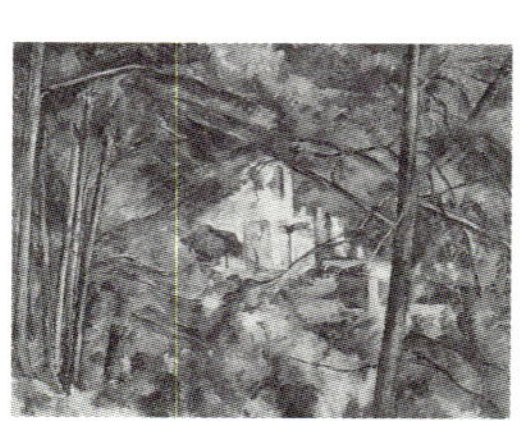

13. *Château Noir.* c. 1894–1895. The Château Noir sits to the east of Aix in view of Mont Sainte-Victoire and other motifs that Cézanne favored during his later years. He offered to buy the Château Noir in 1899; when the owner refused, Cézanne rented studio space there, traveling from the town each day.

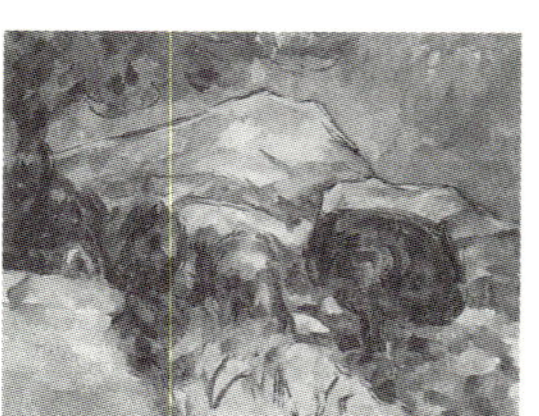

14. *Mont Sainte-Victoire above the Tholonet Road.* c. 1904. This view of the mountain appears along the route that passes the Château Noir. The work is typically unfinished; a later hand may have added the unmodulated areas of gray to make the painting appear more complete and therefore saleable.

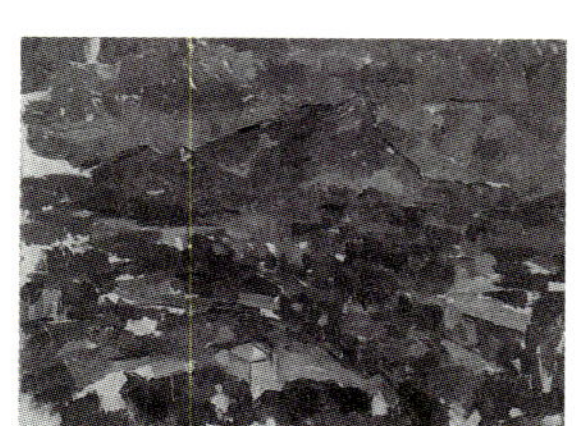

15. *Mont Sainte-Victoire Seen from Les Lauves.* 1902–1906. This view of the mountain can be seen from outside the studio Cézanne built just north of Aix in 1902. The linear accents are fragments of contour that Cézanne added and painted over repeatedly, sometimes causing them to disappear entirely, sometimes to accumulate as a set of thick parallel strokes.

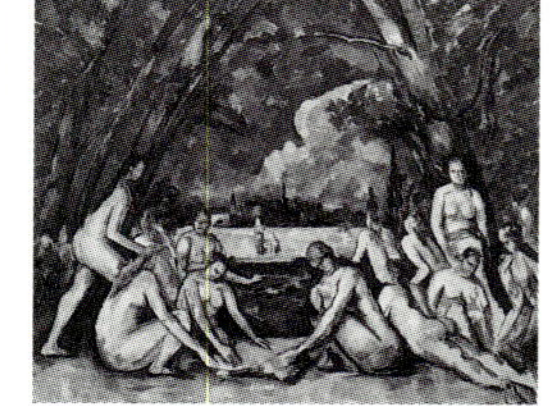

16. *Large Bathers.* 1906. Unfinished at Cézanne's death, this vaguely classical image followed two other large versions of the theme painted during the preceding decade; ultimately it derives from some of Cézanne's earliest compositions. The crouching bather at the left may have acquired its extremely small head because the source Cézanne used was an antique statue having no head at all.

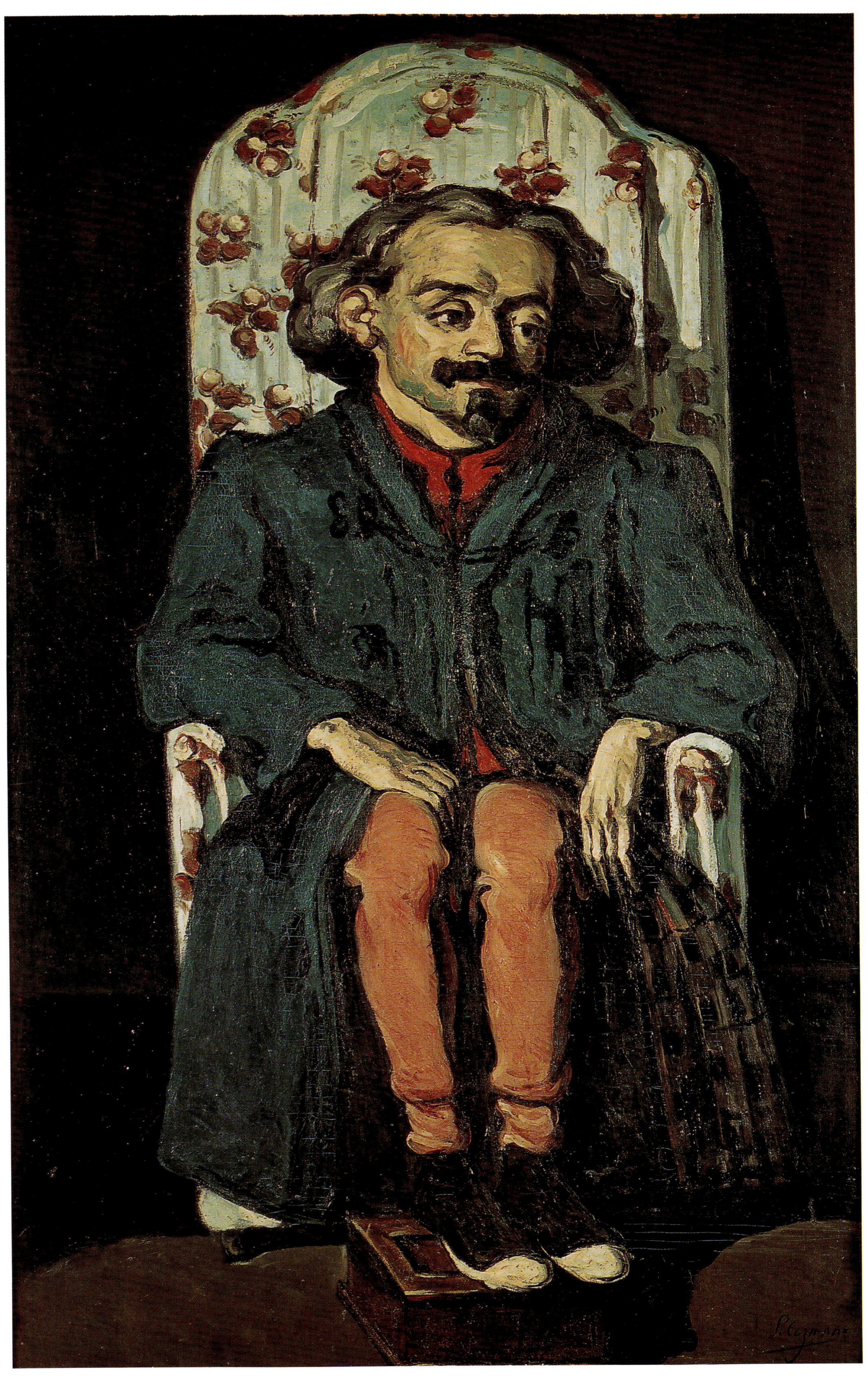

1. *Portrait of Achille Emperaire.* c. 1868–1870. Oil on canvas, 78¾ x 48".
Musée d'Orsay, Paris. Photograph courtesy Réunion des Musées Nationaux

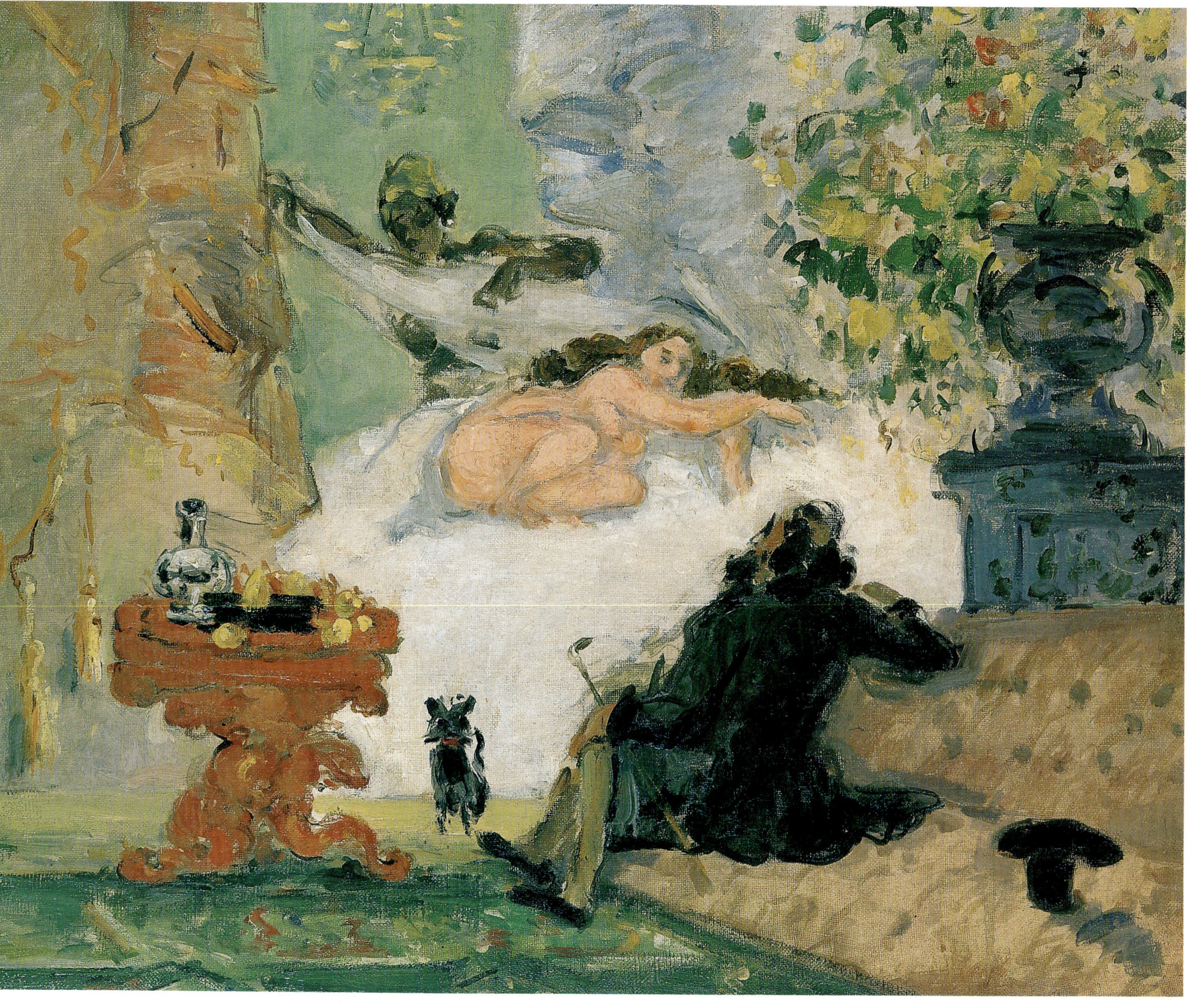

2. *A Modern Olympia*. 1873–1874. Oil on canvas, 18 x 21⅔".
Musée d'Orsay, Paris. Photograph courtesy Réunion des Musées Nationaux

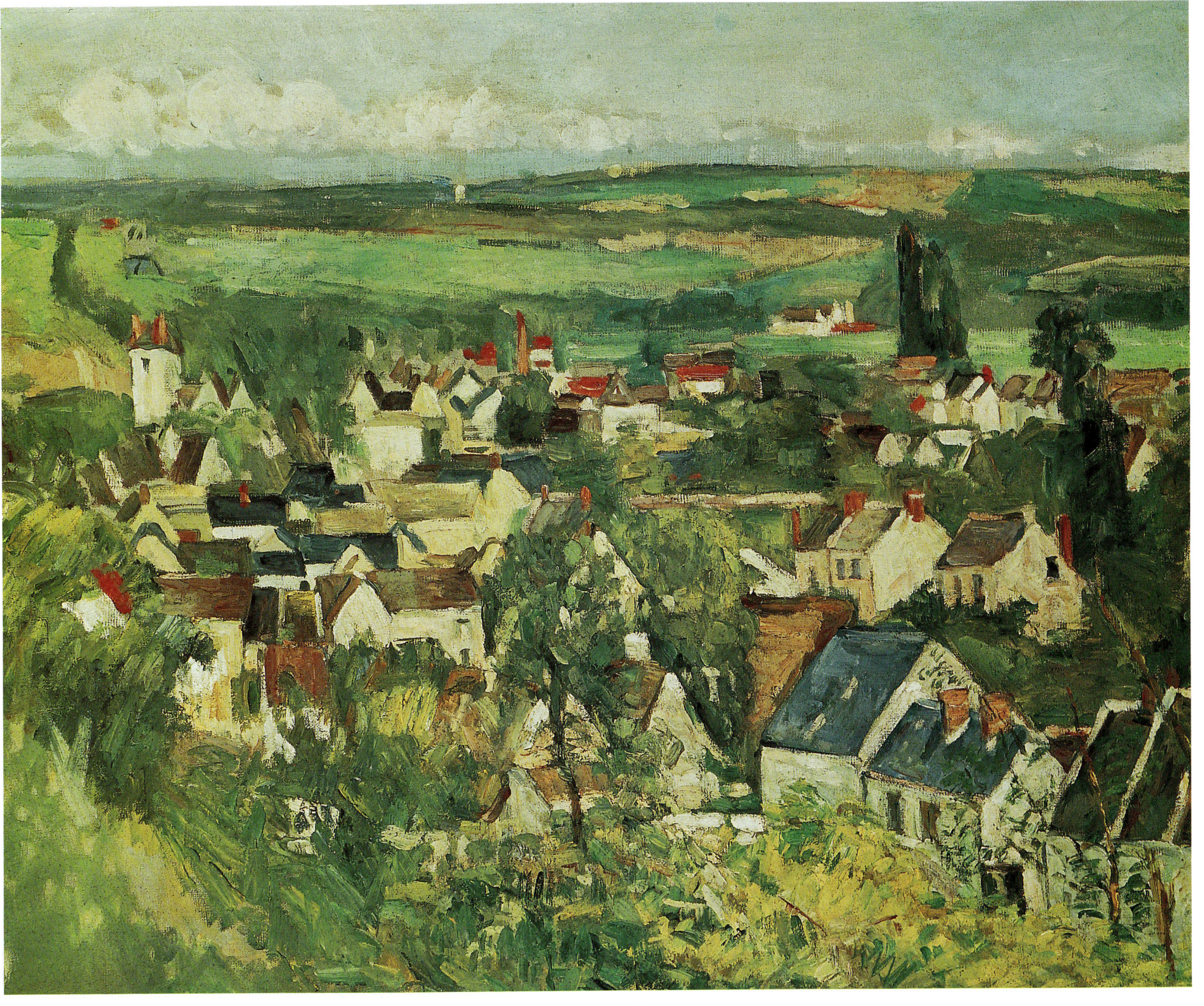

3. *Village of Auvers.* c. 1874. Oil on canvas, 25⅔ x 32".
The Art Institute of Chicago. Mr. and Mrs. Lewis Larned Coburn Memorial Collection (1933.422)

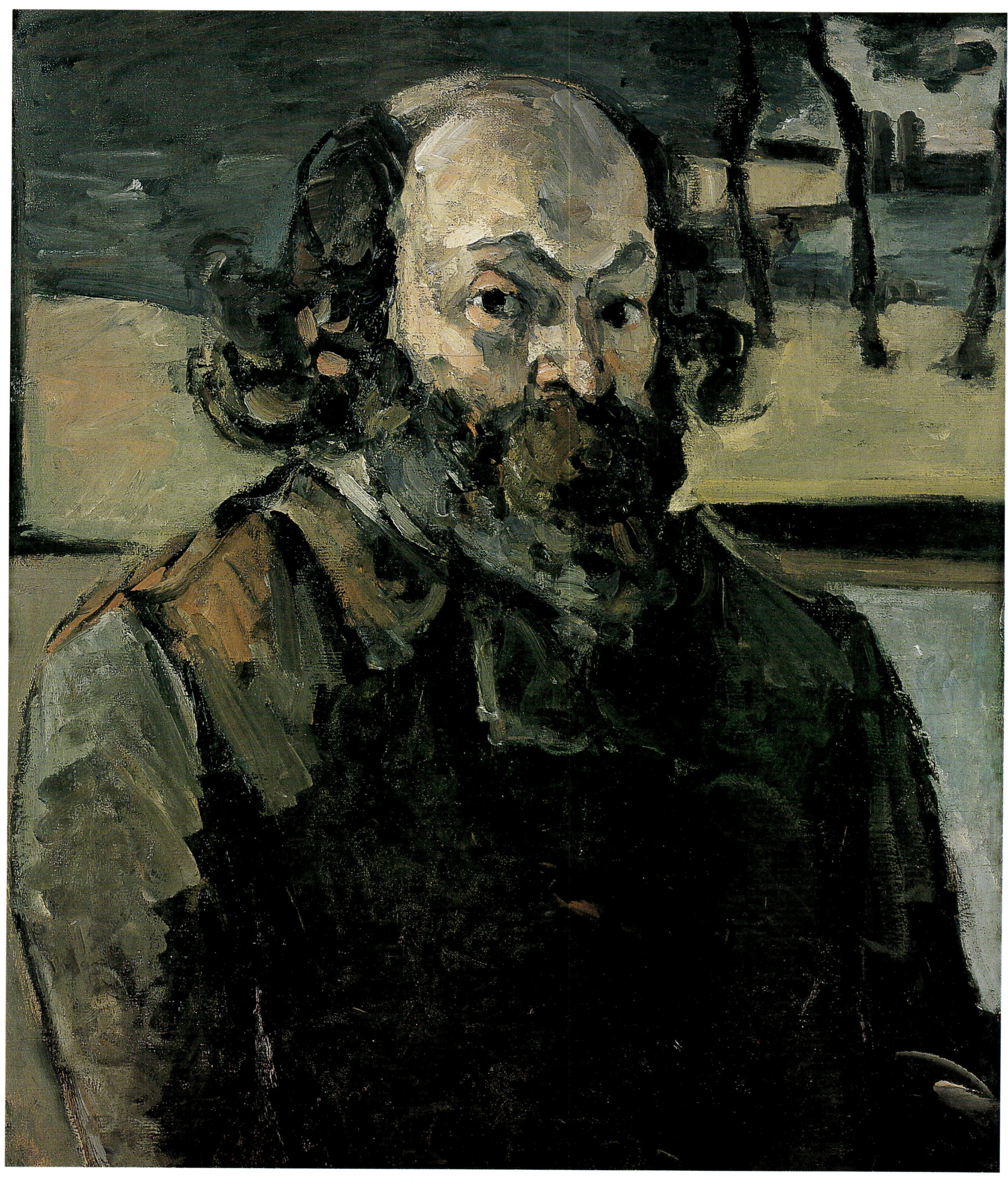

4. *Self-Portrait*. c. 1872. Oil on canvas, 25½ x 21¼".
Musée d'Orsay, Paris. Photograph courtesy Réunion des Musées Nationaux

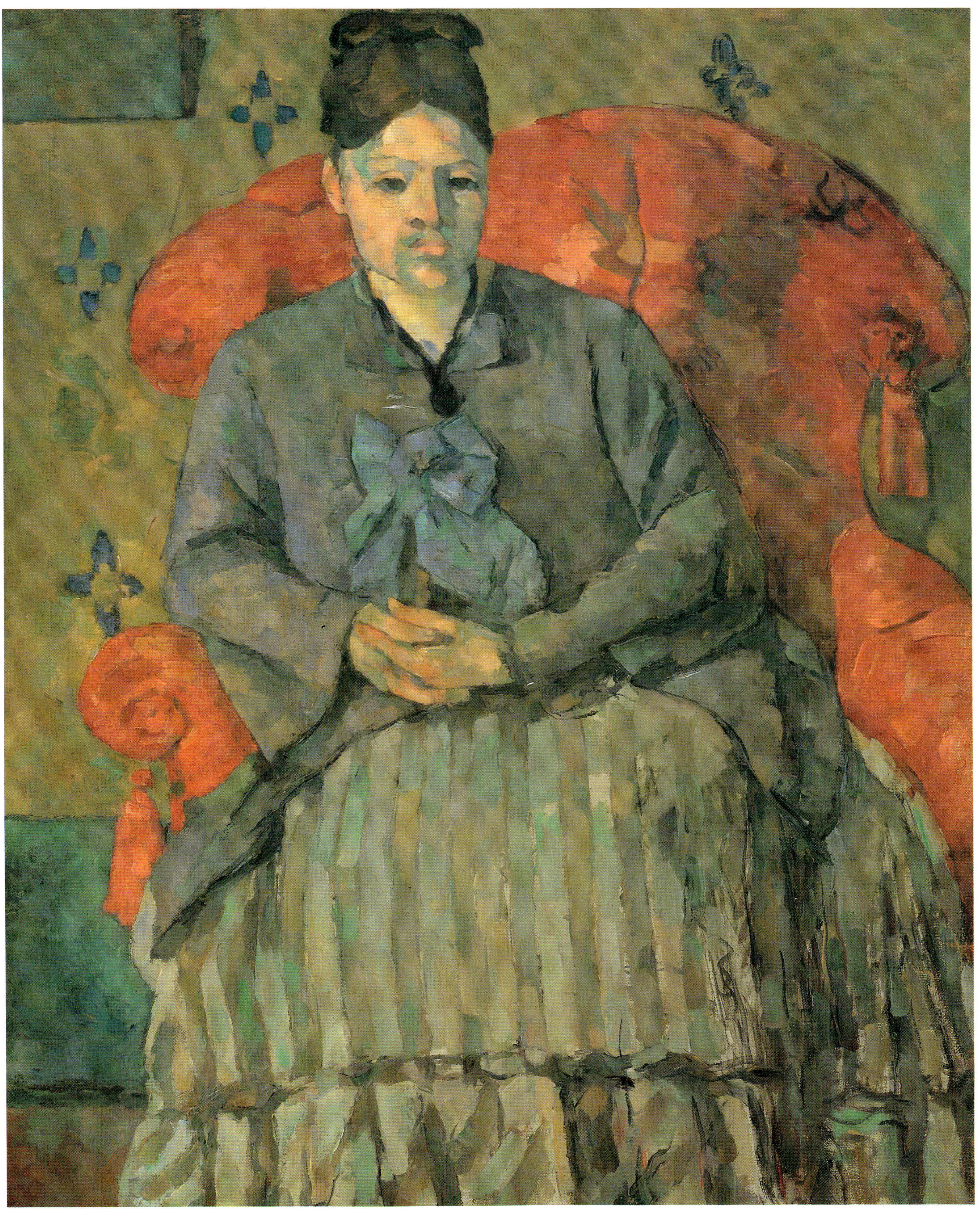

5. *Portrait of Mme Cézanne.* 1877–1878. Oil on canvas, 28½ x 22".
Museum of Fine Arts, Boston. Bequest of Robert Treat Paine II

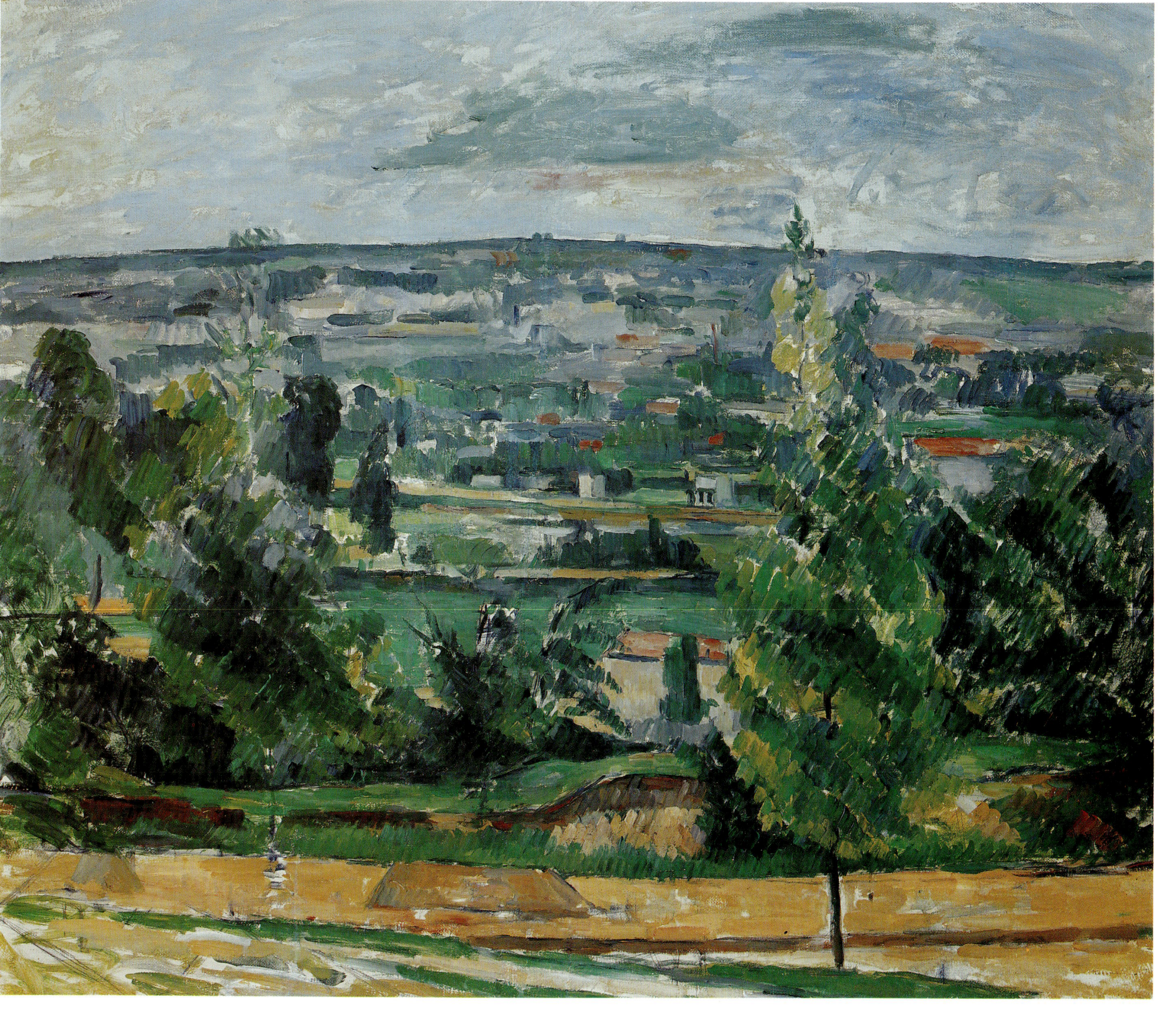

6. *Landscape (near Melun?)*. c. 1879–1882. Oil on canvas, 23⅔ x 28¾".
National Gallery, Oslo. Photograph by J. Lathion

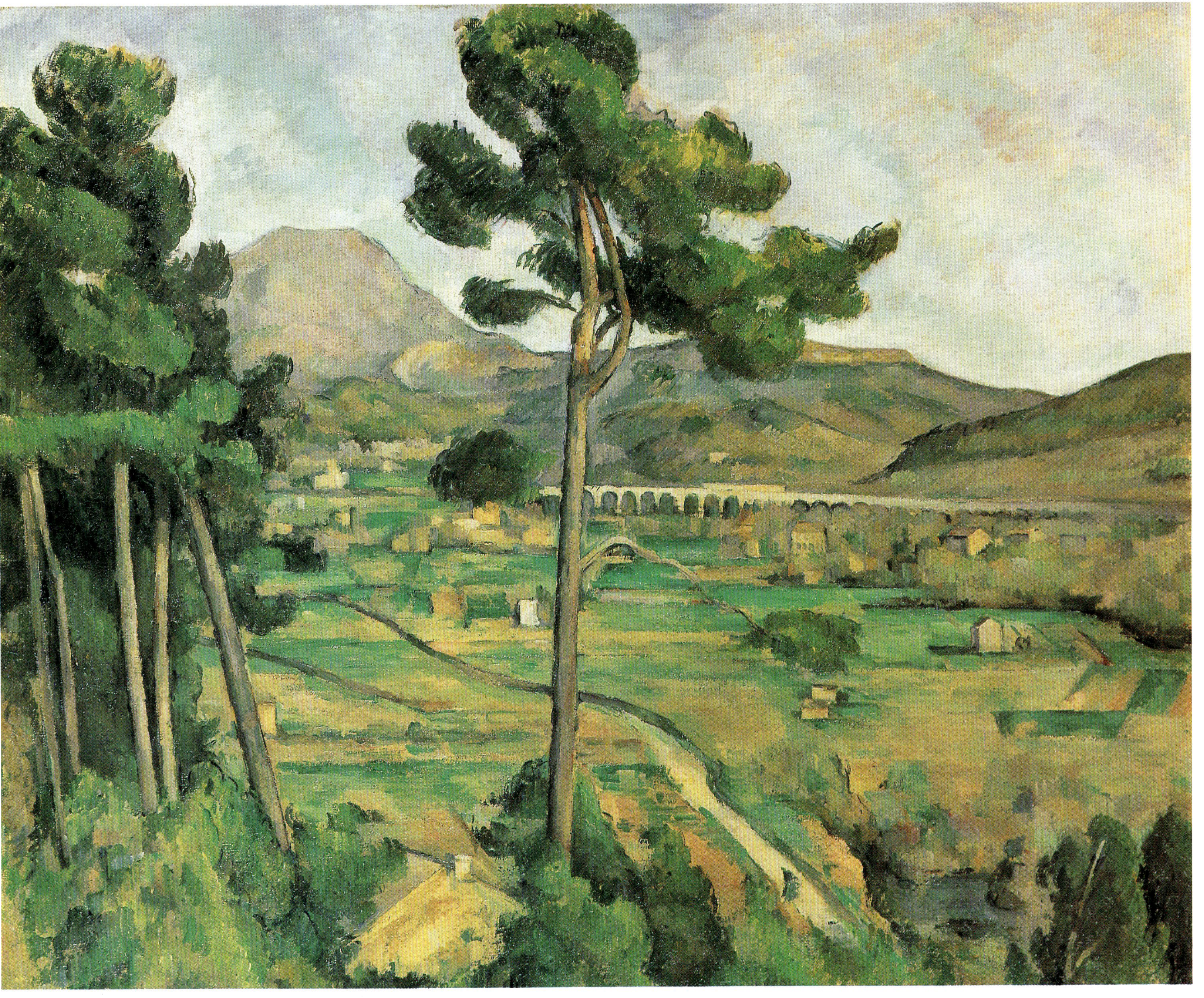

7. *Mont Sainte-Victoire.* c. 1883–1885. Oil on canvas, 25¾ x 32⅛".
The Metropolitan Museum of Art. Bequest of Mrs. H. O. Havemeyer, 1929. The H. O. Havemeyer Collection (29.100.64)

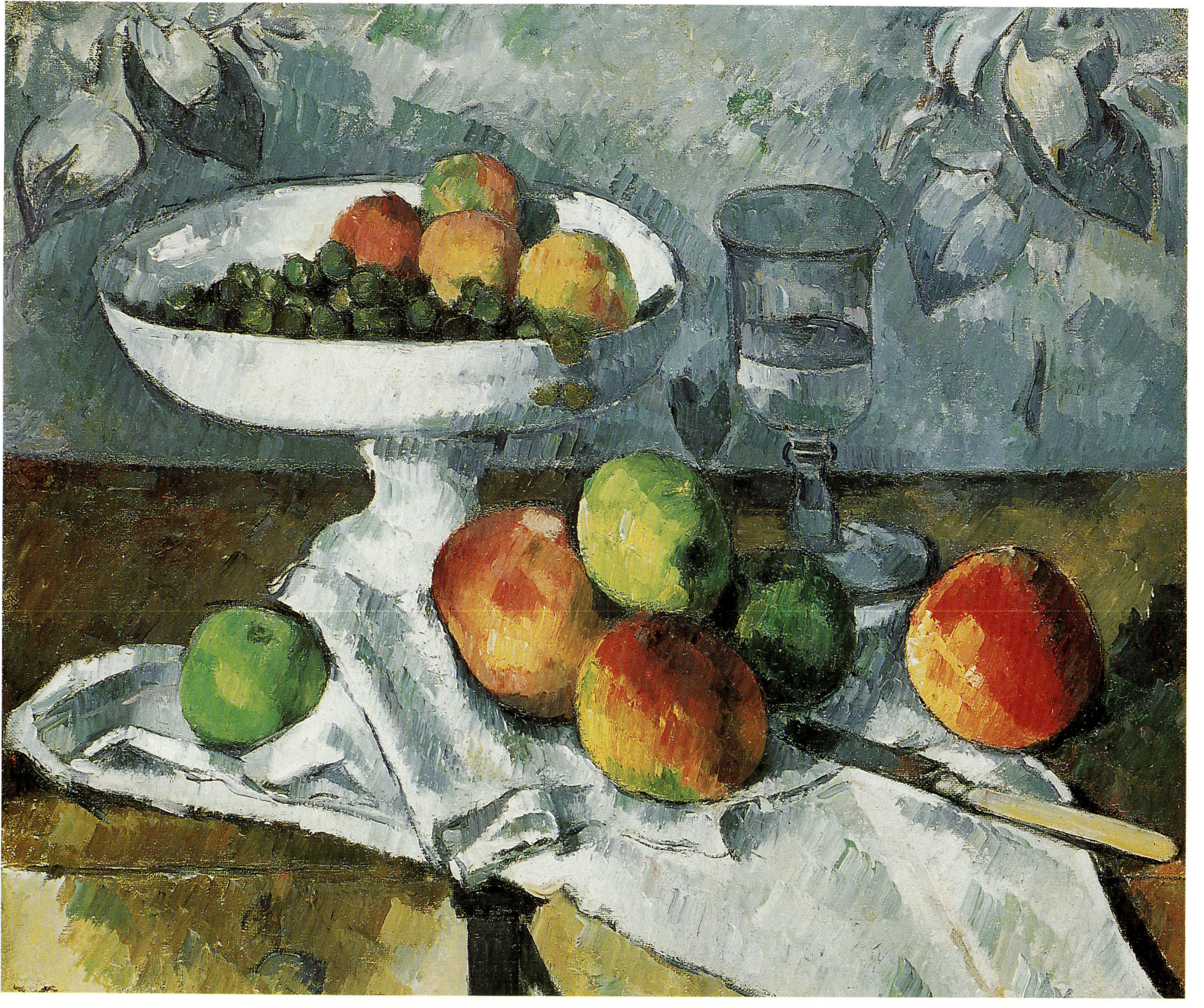

8. *Fruit Bowl, Glass, and Apples*. c. 1880. Oil on canvas, 18⅛ x 21⅝".
Private collection. Photograph by Malcolm Varon, New York

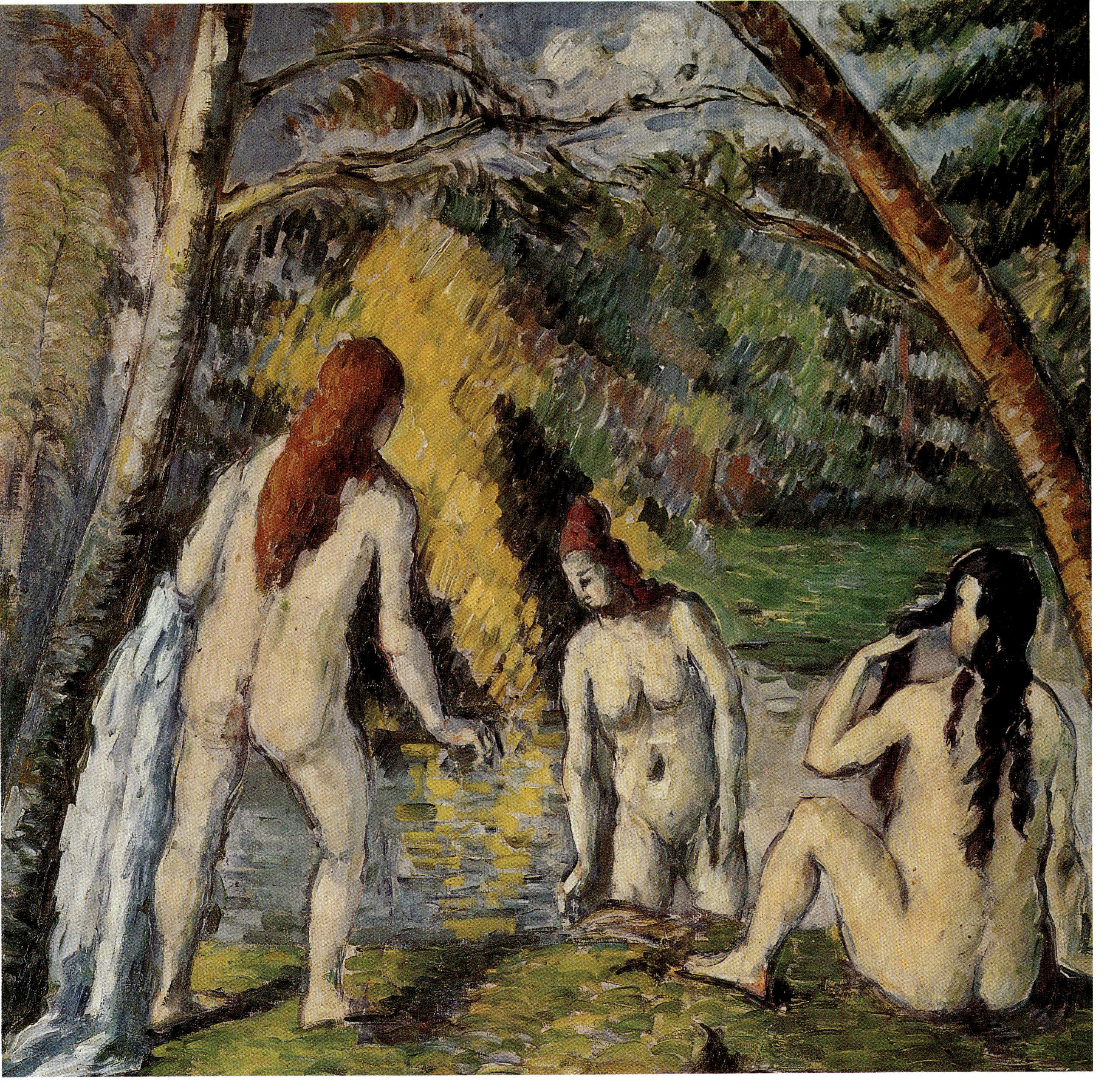

9. *Three Bathers.* c. 1881–1882. Oil on canvas, 22¾ x 21½".
Petit Palais, Paris. Photograph courtesy Giraudon/Art Resource, New York

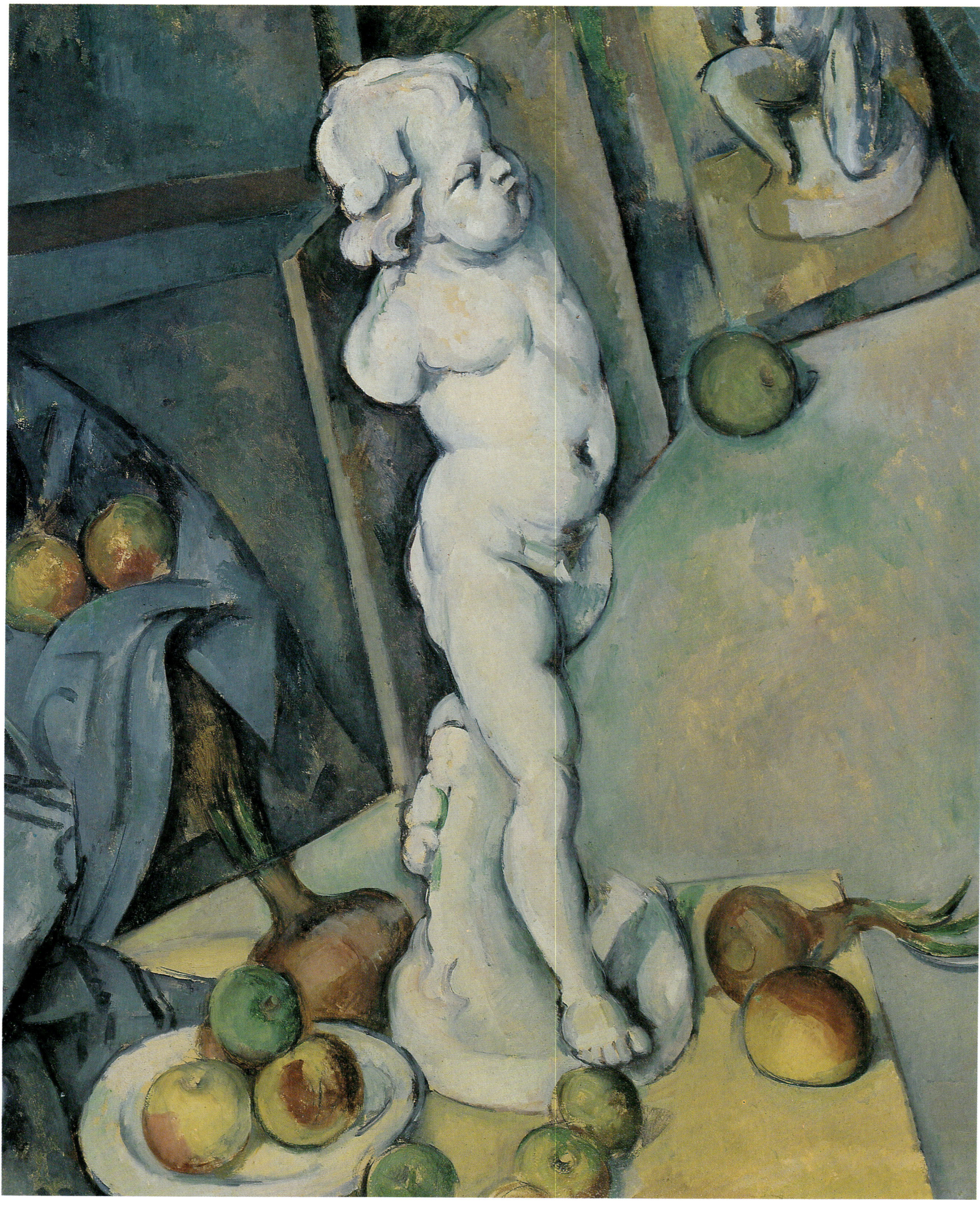

10. *Still Life with Plaster Cupid.* c. 1892–1894. Oil on paper on board, 27$\frac{3}{10}$ x 22$\frac{1}{2}$".
Courtauld Institute Galleries, London

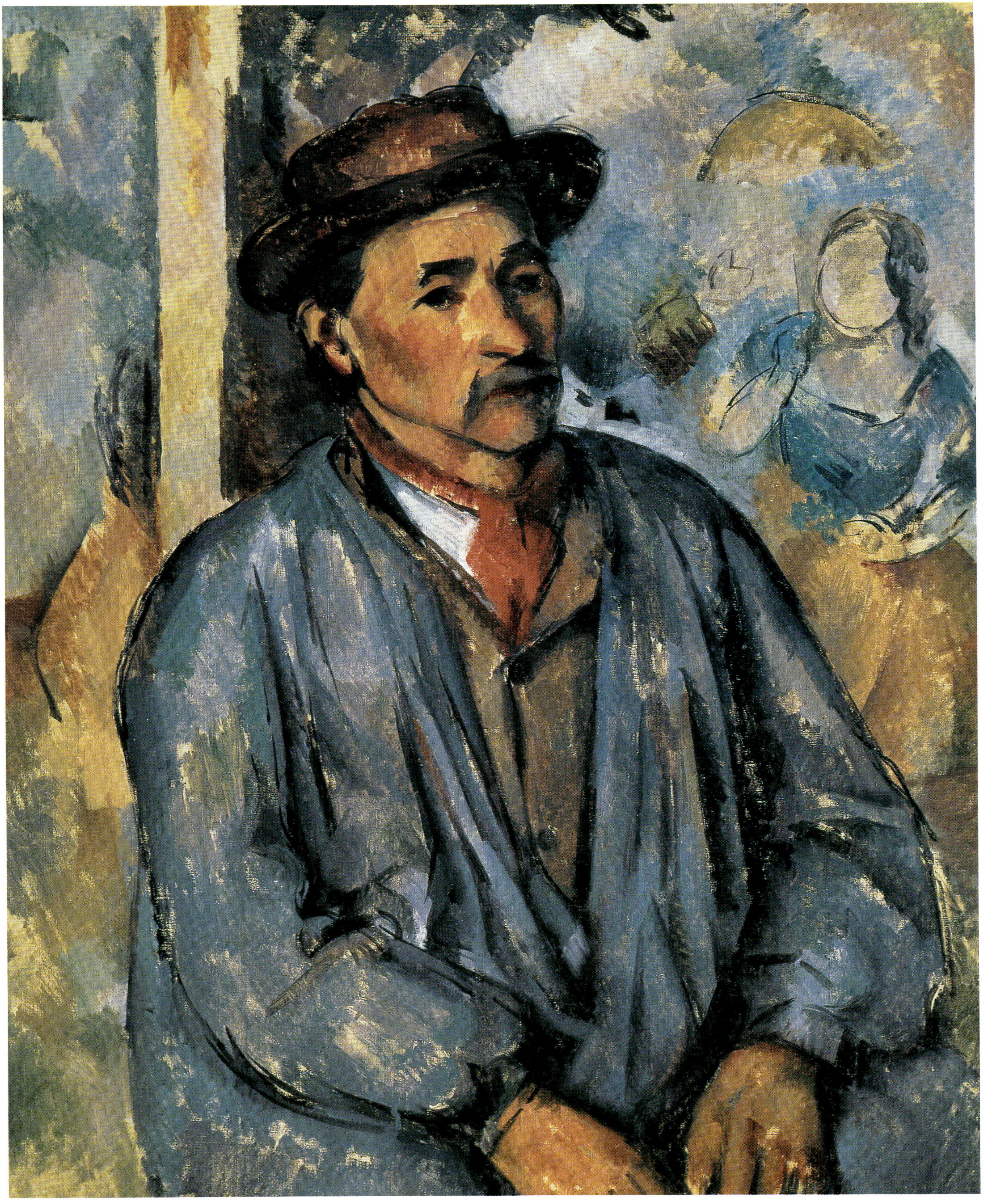

11. *Peasant in a Blue Smock.* c. 1897. Oil on canvas, 32⅛ x 25½".
Kimbell Art Museum, Fort Worth, Texas

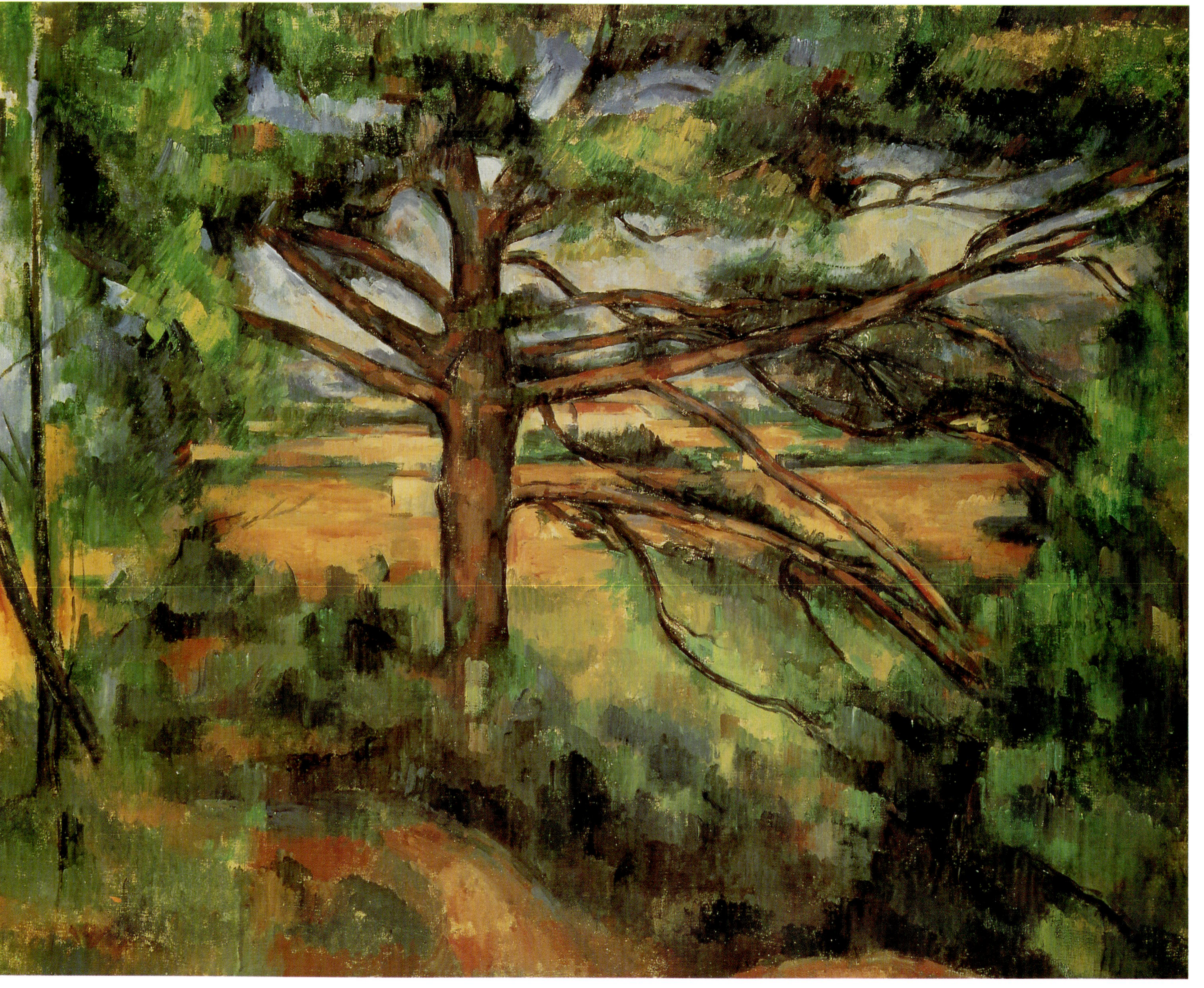

12. *Large Pine Tree near Aix.* c. 1895–1897. $31\frac{9}{10}$ x $39\frac{3}{8}$".
Hermitage Museum, St. Petersburg. Photograph courtesy Scala/Art Resource, New York

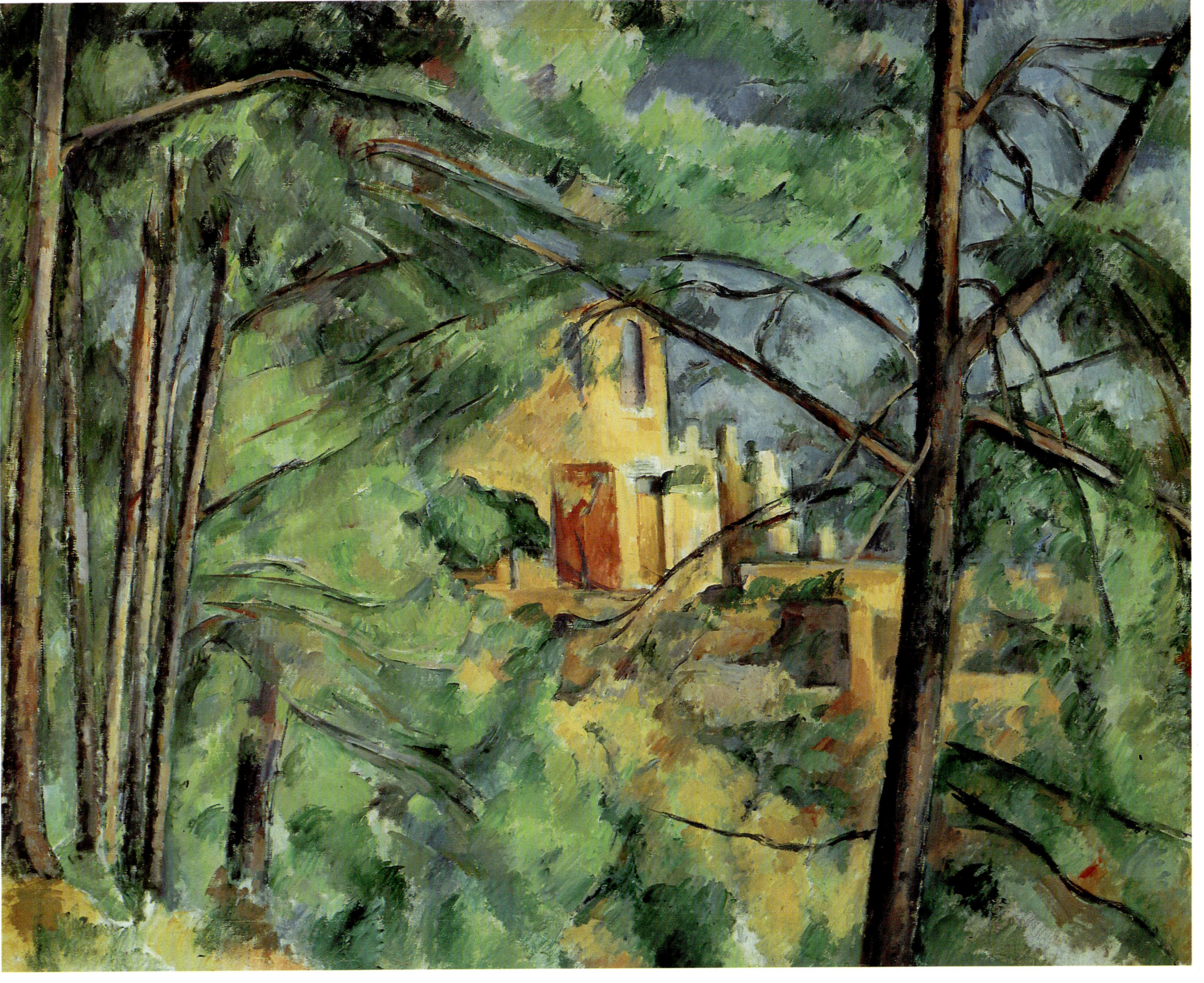

13. *Château Noir.* c. 1894–1895. Oil on canvas, 29 x 36⅜".
Oskar Reinhart Collection "Am Römerholz," Winterthur, Switzerland

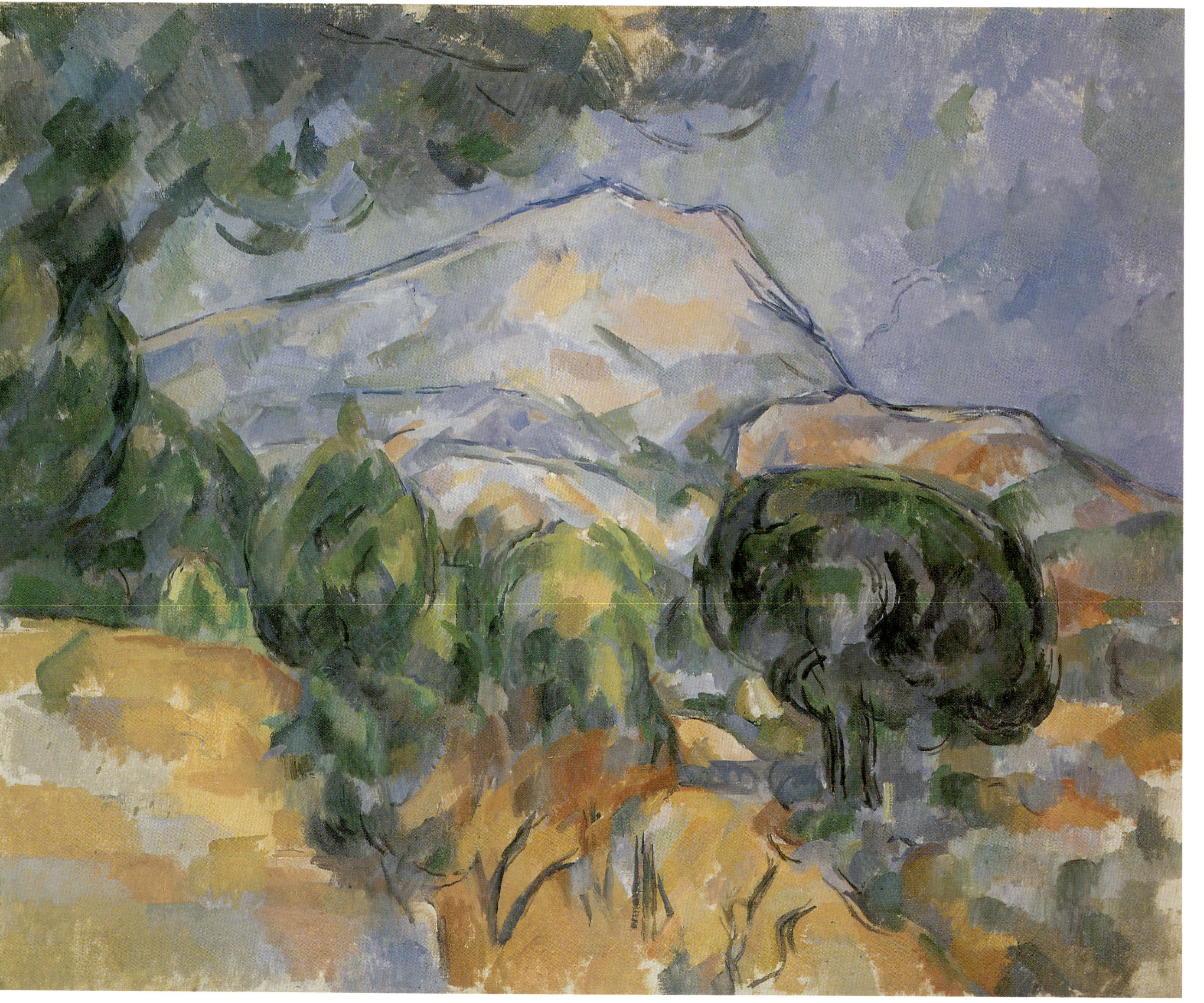

14. *Mont Sainte-Victoire above the Tholonet Road.* c. 1904. Oil on canvas, 28$^{13}/_{16}$ x 36$^{1}/_{4}$".
The Cleveland Museum of Art. Bequest of Leonard C. Hanna, Jr. (58.21)

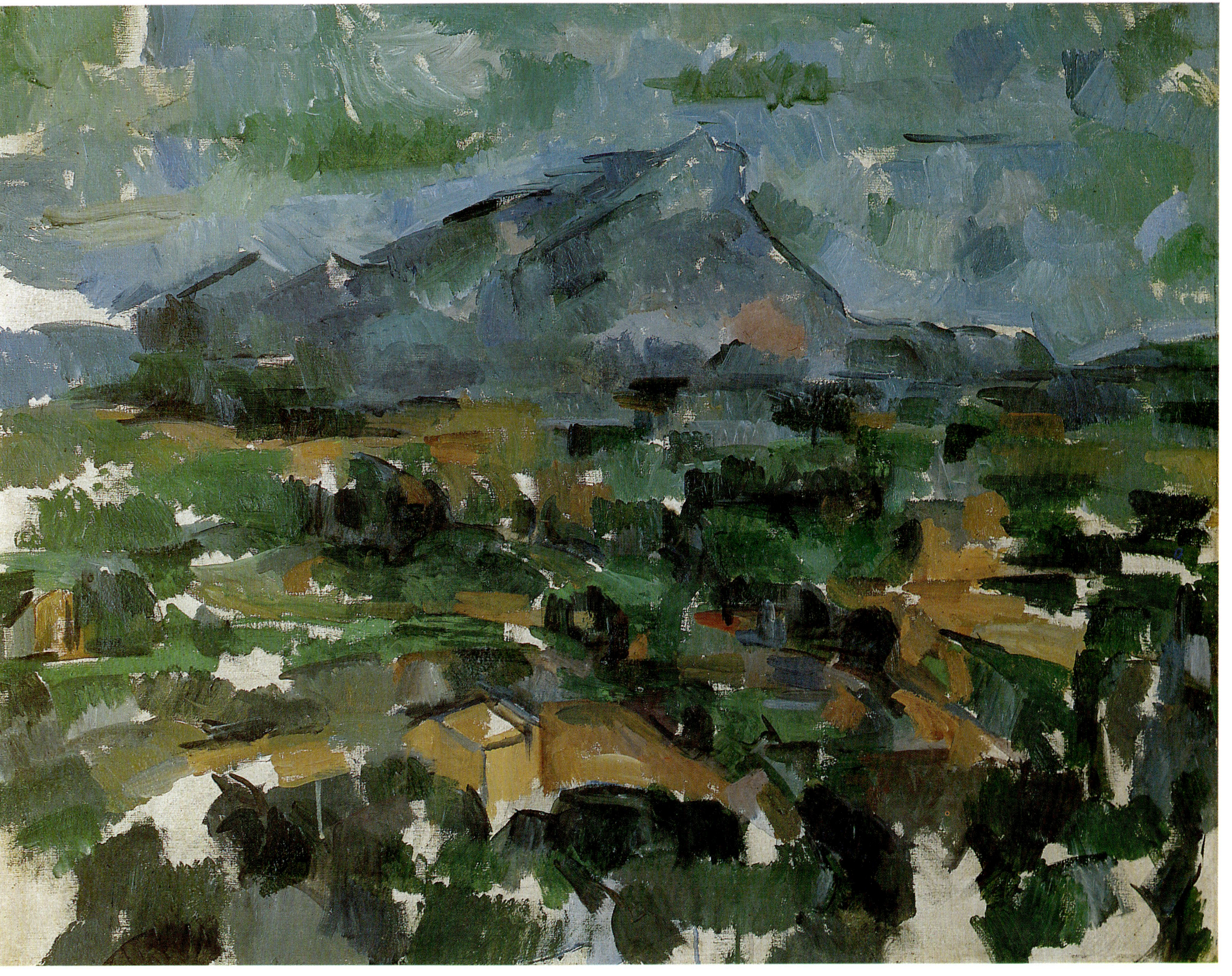

15. *Mont Sainte-Victoire Seen from Les Lauves.* 1902–1906. Oil on canvas. 25 x 32¾".
Kunsthaus Zürich

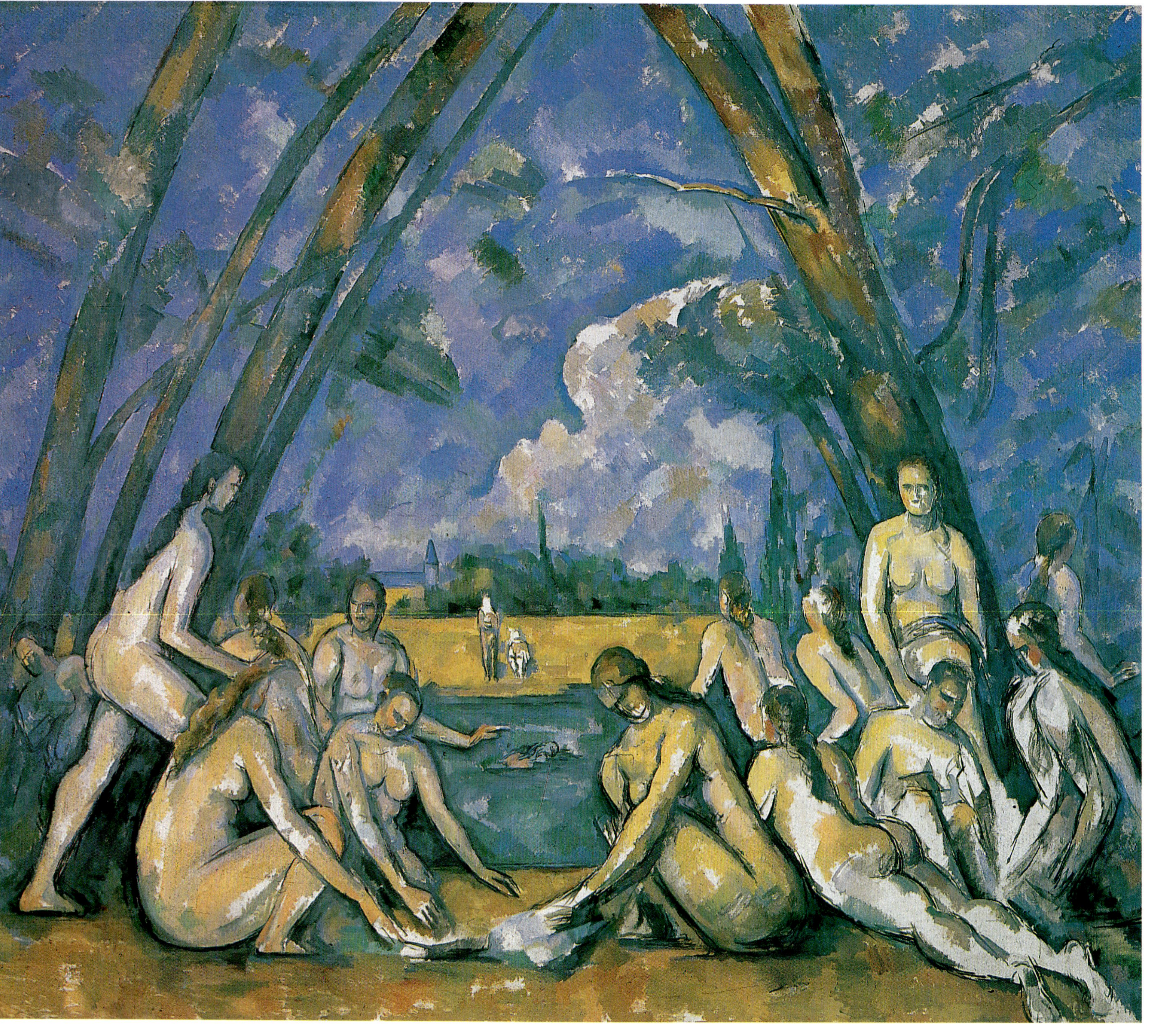

16. *Large Bathers.* 1906. Oil on canvas, 82 x 99".
Philadelphia Museum of Art. The W. P. Wilstach Collection